BURNOUT PAINS

BURNOUT PAINS

A Guide to Prevent Burnout, Rediscover Your Purpose, and Renew Your Energy

DR. REGGIE THOMAS

Burnout Pains: *A Guide to Prevent Burnout, Rediscover Your Purpose, and Renew Your Energy*

Jones Media Publishing
10645 N. Tatum Blvd. Ste. 200-166
Phoenix, AZ 85028
JonesMediaPublishing.com

Printed in the United States of America

ISBN: 978-1-948382-86-1 paperback

Thanks for reading!

Get an exclusive interview with
Dr. Reggie Thomas about how to avoid burnout.

Get it here:

PeoplePains.com

TABLE OF CONTENTS

Foreword ix

Introduction xiii

CHAPTER 1: What Is Burnout? 1

CHAPTER 2: Causes of Burnout. 15

CHAPTER 3: Managing Job Burnout 37

CHAPTER 4: The Symptoms of Burnout 61

CHAPTER 5: How to Prevent Burnout 81

CHAPTER 6: How to Recover from Burnout. . . 101

Becoming Fulfilled 127

Author Bio 137

FOREWORD

This book couldn't have come at a better time. As an Executive Coach, Leadership Consultant, and former COO, I see the symptoms of burnout nearly every day. That's because burnout doesn't discriminate on factors such as age, gender, or ethnicity. It affects all kinds of professionals at all levels of their careers, across all sectors and industries.

Burnout is just as serious as Dr. Reggie Thomas describes. Personally, it wreaks havoc on our mental, emotional, and physical health. Professionally, it stunts our effectiveness and productivity at work. Burnout harms our relationships, our mindset, and our zest for life. And, for whatever reason, we don't talk about it enough. There simply isn't enough awareness of what burnout truly is, and how to address it. Perhaps we're unaware. Perhaps we're *afraid*.

In this fascinating book, Reggie approaches the topic of burnout through a multitude of lenses. He openly shares personal stories that detail the causes and symptoms of burnout, numerous prevention techniques, and actionable ideas for how to recover from burnout. His stories are vivid and real, and you'll likely recognize yourself (or someone you know) in the characters and their experiences. If you're experiencing burnout, this book will help you identify it. You'll find comfort in the stories and you will no longer feel so alone.

You'll also find valuable suggestions to address what you're feeling and how to move forward. Reggie tackles critically important topics such as practicing self-care, setting and enforcing boundaries, time and self-management, and exuding courage. This book offers its readers strategies for overcoming learned behaviors that affect many of us. For those of us who have Type A personalities or were raised to be perfectionists, people-pleasers, and high-achievers, this book will invigorate you. It reminds us we have choices in how we manage those tendencies and that it's never too late to develop new practices and principles for managing ourselves and our careers. In that regard, this book is full of hope.

This book's sound advice is universal. Reggie's practical applications are extremely relevant in all walks of life, including work, home, and/or extracurricular activities. Reggie reminds us that different individuals experience burnout differently. Perhaps you've felt tired or exhausted. Perhaps you've felt stressed or overwhelmed. Perhaps you've felt bored and listless. Regardless of what you're personally experiencing, this book will give you the tools and techniques to reclaim your mood and your life.

Perhaps the best thing about this book is the author himself. There is no one more equipped than Dr. Reggie Thomas to write this book. Not only has Reggie both experienced and recovered from burnout himself, but he's also studied and researched the topic extensively. Reggie's willingness to be humble and vulnerable in this book, for the sake of our learning and growth, is a truly brave act. But, Reggie goes the extra mile by combining his personal learnings with an incredible amount of data and anecdotal evidence. Numerous studies are cited and referenced throughout this book, making it an academic and educational work, as well. This self-help book strikes the ideal balance between relatable personal memoir and informative textbook.

It's always exciting to learn from veritable experts. Perhaps one of the most enjoyable aspects of this book is knowing that Reggie practices what he preaches. Today, Reggie is an experienced and highly sought speaker and business consultant. After dealing with his own burnout, he made the tough decision to build his own business with his bare hands. He's done what many of us wish we could do. He also invests heavily in his personal life. He spends ample time with his wife, two daughters, and extended family. He's an avid marathon runner, completing the prestigious Boston Marathon 12 times. He travels extensively, gardens, reads, and has made time to write two transformational books. When it comes to the risk of burnout that we all face, Reggie models what success looks like.

Similar to burnout, this book is universal in its relevance. It caters to readers of all ages and is particularly beneficial for professionals navigating fast-paced or high-stress environments. You'll find immense value in its insights. Additionally, leaders and managers overseeing teams should prioritize its consumption. Your employees will appreciate the investment in their well-being.

– Amy Chambers

Amy Chambers is a multifaceted professional, serving as an Executive Coach, Life Coach, Leadership Consultant, Speaker, and Author. She has authored two bestselling books on Amazon: "7 V.I.R.T.U.E.S. of Exceptional Leaders" and "6 H.A.B.I.T.S. of Powerful People," both reaching the #1 spot in their respective categories.

INTRODUCTION

The idea of writing this book had been percolating in my head for a while. My reason for actually taking the leap and writing it stemmed from overcoming my own bout of burnout. My aim is to share my story and journey in hopes that it will encourage you—whether you're heading towards burnout, in the middle of it, or coming out on the other side. As you read through this book, you'll sense my honesty and openness, getting the unfiltered truth about my experience with raw emotion and transparency.

Not only do I want to share the narrative of my burnout experience; I also want to share my learnings, including various concepts and principles that will help you to prevent and recover from burnout.

Sadly, burnout is on the rise. In fact, it has become an epidemic in the workplace, affecting not only organizational leaders but also employees across the board. Statistics show it peaked in 2023, significantly impacting businesses as employees resign, lose motivation, and consequently reduce morale and productivity in the workplace.

Many organizational leaders are taking it seriously, as they should. From creating support systems that provide opportunities for employee wellbeing and self-care to implementing healthy workplace boundaries, managers need to take action to help employees prevent burnout. According to the American Psychological Association's 2021 Work and Wellbeing Survey, 3 in 5 workers reported experiencing negative mental and physical impacts due to work related stress. It also showed 26% noted a lack of interest, motivation or energy, while 32% reported emotional exhaustion, and 44% said they feel high levels of physical fatigue.

I have two main objectives for writing this book. The first is to help managers understand the seriousness of burnout syndrome, enabling them to offer support to their teams and establish systems that can prevent burnout among employees. The second is for this book to serve as a resource for any employee who is currently experiencing burnout. Whether you're just starting to feel its effects or you're already at your breaking point, I hope the concepts presented here will help you halt the decline. Additionally, for those deeply entrenched in burnout, I'll share tools to aid in your recovery.

Burnout is often misunderstood, with many people unaware of its true nature and severity. I'll delve deeper into this in the first chapter. Despite focusing on the negative aspects of this epidemic, this book is ultimately about hope. It's possible to prevent burnout and achieve full recovery from it.

Now, before I dive into the chapters, I want to give you an overview of my journey and personal experiences. As I move through each chapter, I will refer back to portions of my story, adding more details along the way.

It all began in 2018. At the time, I was the Business Administrator of a church and served as the number two guy on staff. Juggling responsibilities such as managing staff, operations, programming, budgeting, finances, and overseeing administration, I began feeling fatigued, experiencing a loss of passion for my work, and a decline in energy come springtime. These sensations weren't unfamiliar to me; I'd encountered them before in my career. However, a simple vacation was usually enough to pull me out of my funk, leaving me renewed, refreshed, and ready to tackle any task at hand.

That summer, my wife and I took an amazing vacation to Italy. From Venice to Rome, we explored all the historical sites and had a great time, as usual. However, as our vacation neared its end, I realized I wasn't looking forward to going back to work. In fact, I felt a sense of dread at the thought of resuming my job responsibilities.

Back at work, I still felt tired, emotionally drained and utterly depleted. The vacation didn't help my condition at all. I immediately recognized that what I was experiencing went beyond the need for a fun, relaxing break to recharge – I wasn't recharged at all.

Throughout 2018, I managed to conceal my feelings from everyone. Despite how I felt, I continued to perform my job well. It never occurred to me at the time that I might be experiencing burnout. I didn't even want to entertain that possibility. In my mind, burnout was something that only affected the "weak" or other leaders, not someone like me. So, I soldiered on, going through the motions, but it took a toll. I hoped that what I was feeling would improve or disappear over time. Unfortunately, it didn't.

I entered 2019 and the emotional slide increased. My burnout symptoms worsened, but still, I refused to admit I might be in burnout. Not only was I mentally exhausted, but I also started experiencing physical fatigue and sleep problems. There were nights when falling asleep was a struggle, and I'd often wake up in the middle of the night unable to get back to sleep. Some nights, it felt like I hadn't slept at all. Naturally, this began to impact my focus and concentration during the day.

I scheduled an appointment with my doctor and discussed my insomnia issue with him. I asked if he could prescribe sleep medication to help me. After a discussion, he cautioned me about the potential major side effects of certain sleep medications and suggested trying Trazodone instead, an *anti-anxiety medication* that has been proven to help with sleep issues. Each night, I would pop a Trazodone tablet about an hour before going to bed. At first, it helped, but after a while, it no longer worked. That was the first time I was willing to get real and admit to myself I was in burnout. It wasn't solely due to the physical symptoms; there were other signs indicating this as well.

During this time, I also felt extreme emotional exhaustion. I found myself devoid of passion for my 30-year career in professional ministry, especially in my role as the Business Administrator. Getting out of bed became a struggle, and the mere thought of going to work filled me with dread. Nearly every aspect of my job felt like a burden. Despite being a professional with years of experience, I struggled to carry out my duties. Phone calls, meetings, and conversations felt like a chore, and I approached them with reluctance and frustration.

It has been said that insanity is doing the same thing over and over again and expecting different results. Determined not to give in, my stubborn nature led me to attempt the vacation strategy once more. In 2019, my wife and I embarked on two international trips, visiting Israel in the winter and Spain in the summer. However, both times, I returned to work feeling the same physical and emotional exhaustion. Activities that once brought me joy now left me feeling indifferent. As the problem solver on the church staff, my role as the Business Administrator of a large church presented numerous challenges, particularly in managing conflicts and resolving issues. While I had previously handled these tasks well emotionally, the constant demands of problem-solving and conflict resolution began to take a toll on me. Gradually, I found myself despising my job.

Having grown up in Tennessee, in the fall of 2019, I made a short trip back to visit family. Specifically, I flew to Memphis, where an old college friend lived. Upon landing, we arranged to meet at a restaurant, where I confided in him about what was going on in my life. Our conversation turned out to be a moment of revelation for me. He pointed out that I was experiencing deep burnout and suggested that perhaps the responsibilities of my current position weren't aligning with my passions. Honestly, I didn't know how to process this information. However, it proved to be enlightening, sparking a profound sense of awareness within me.

I was truly fried by the time 2020 rolled around. That year, one of my first duties was to conduct performance reviews for my direct reports. I directly supervised a team of ten staff members, with my performance review conducted by the Senior Pastor. As part of our review process, we were required to complete a self-evaluation. In mine, I briefly mentioned experiencing burnout, but I downplayed its severity. Pride and fear of job loss prevented me from fully acknowledging the extent of my struggle. During the review meeting, when the Senior Pastor addressed it, I brushed it off, saying, "It's not that serious, so I'll be okay." Looking back, I realize this was a significant mistake. It was a missed opportunity to seek the support I needed to begin the process of recovery.

In March, when the COVID shutdown occurred and we transitioned to remote work, my downward spiral intensified. It reached a point where I felt compelled to seek help, leading me to schedule a lunch meeting with the chairman of the board. During our conversation, I opened up about my burnout struggles, using that exact term. While he didn't know how to respond, he did encourage me to speak with the Senior Pastor. Recognizing the urgency of my situation, I decided I needed a sabbatical or leave of absence to recover. In an honest conversation with the Senior Pastor, I expressed my desire for a ten-week sabbatical. Although this decision wasn't well-received from a career standpoint, I knew it was essential for my well-being. Recovering from burnout isn't something that happens overnight; it requires deliberate effort and intentionality. I understood what needed to be done for my own recovery.

I prepared a document outlining burnout, citing statistics, and describing my feelings. In the proposal, I suggested a 10-week sabbatical without pay, fearing the board wouldn't grant it at all if I'd asked for it with pay. Later you will learn that they actually took me up on the "without pay" part! This proposal was emailed to the board, and a meeting was convened on Memorial Day evening, where I addressed the board and requested the sabbatical.

I was excused from the board meeting so they could discuss the proposal. I expected to hear from the Senior Pastor or the chairman of the board the next morning. If approved, I planned to start the sabbatical after two or three weeks to coordinate a communication and transition plan with the board, staff, and leaders. That night, I went to bed expecting to have those conversations the next day.

However, at midnight, I received a call from the chairman of the board. Surprised by the timing,

I answered and he immediately informed me of the approval without pay, to begin immediately. I politely challenged this, suggesting a delayed start, but he insisted it must commence right away and that I shouldn't report to work the next day.

This part of the story is crucial, underscoring the severity of my burnout. Upon ending the call, I felt a wave of relief wash over me. The weight of responsibility lifted, yet fear lingered as I knew burnout recovery in church settings sometimes led to termination. Despite this, I fell asleep feeling liberated and relieved, waking up with a newfound sense of freedom.

I spent the first day of my sabbatical reflecting on what I would do during the next ten weeks to recover from my burnout. I devised a plan comprising of reading, forming a support group, seeking professional guidance, and reflecting on life post-burnout.

Though nerve-wracking at the time, I can honestly say now that I made the right decision. I spent that time resting, reflecting, processing and even praying about where I was in life and what the road to recovery would look like. Each day, I slept in, took naps throughout the day, spent time with my family, exercised, read, and checked in with my support team, who encouraged me, held me accountable and helped me process my condition.

At the end of my sabbatical, the board decided I was no longer a fit and terminated me "without cause." I was surprised–but not that surprised. Sure, the board members were longtime friends and I had been a dedicated, loyal, and effective staff member. However, I sensed the board didn't understand burnout. I'll delve further into this in a later chapter, discussing the potential trajectory of life and career post-recovery from burnout. For me, experiencing burnout and subsequent termination sparked a redirection and repurposing of my life.

Despite my termination, it wasn't a negative event; rather, it served as a catalyst for significant positive changes in my life. If you're grappling with burnout, I hope that by learning more about my experience, you'll realize you're not alone. It doesn't have to consume you; instead, it can be a transformative experience that guides you towards a life filled with passion, fulfillment, and purpose. Through my two-year journey, I've learned valuable lessons that I'm eager to share in the upcoming chapters. These insights will not only help you prevent burnout but also guide you through the process of recovery.

CHAPTER 1

WHAT IS BURNOUT?

I first heard the term "burnout" in the 1990s, but I really didn't understand it. I certainly didn't believe I would ever experience it. Once I stumbled upon the term, it didn't take long before I started hearing others talk about feeling burned out. At first, I saw it as a sign of weakness or an indication of deep emotional struggles.

One of the things I've learned about life is there are some things we cannot fully understand until we go through them. Having gone through my own burnout experience, I've gained a newfound ability to empathize with others who are facing similar challenges in the workplace. Now, when I hear fellow professionals sharing their stories, I can connect with them on a deeper level, offering empathy and understanding without any hint of judgment.

The actual term "burnout" originated in the 1970s, coined by American psychologist, Herbert Freudenberger. At that time, it was used to describe medical professionals who felt "burned out" from their tireless and diligent work. Over the years, burnout has evolved to include anyone in a "helping" profession such as counselors, therapists, ministers, and social workers. Burnout can also be a *compassion*-related condition. One way to define compassion is having sympathy, pity, and concern for the sufferings or misfortunes of others.

If you are in a helping or caring profession, you are not just *physically* doing a job. This type of labor is emotionally intensive. Having spent 30 years in a helping profession, I understand the emotional exhaustion that comes with investing in people who are dealing with the sufferings of life. In professions like these, burning out often stems from an inability to disconnect and a failure to prioritize self-care.

Of course, burnout isn't limited to those in helping professions. It's an epidemic happening across all industries. In our modern society, it can happen to anyone, regardless of their chosen profession.

Burnout statistics have shown high rates over the past three years due in part to the pandemic. Returning to my narrative from the introduction of this book, the pace of burnout accelerated significantly during the initial phase of the pandemic. I found myself in the burnout zone back in 2018, failing to address it promptly, and it only worsened as the pandemic unfolded. My experience isn't unique; it mirrors a pattern we've witnessed over the last three years.

Burnout Is Real

A study conducted by Indeed revealed that while more than half (52%) of workers reported feeling burned out, there is a disconnect between the age groups. While just 31% of baby boomers admitted to experiencing burnout, a striking 59% of millennials and 58% of Gen Z respondents reported feeling the same.

Here are a few more study findings:

- In 2021, Mental Health UK revealed that 46% of workers felt more prone to extreme levels of stress compared to the year before, while 1 in 5 reported feeling unable to manage stress and pressure in the workplace.
- A 2022 survey of 15,000 workers across 15 countries by McKinsey Health found that 25% of employees experienced burnout symptoms.
- A Mental Health America and FlexJobs study pointed out that workplace stress affects their mental health and 75% experienced burnout.

- Qualtrics found that 79% of workers across 26 countries felt "at or beyond workload capacity" in 2020.
- This one is really interesting! A higher percentage of women leaders (43%) report feeling burned out compared to men at their level (31%).

What's truly alarming is the finding from the Gallup 2023 State of the Global Workplace Report, indicating that despite the world's recovery from the pandemic's impact, employees continue to endure record-high stress levels.

It's clear that burnout is an epidemic, reaching all-time highs—but the needle isn't moving in the right direction. Because burnout is such a prevalent issue, it's crucial that we raise more awareness and begin to take action. I believe both employees and employers share the responsibility. As an employee, prioritizing your well-being and practicing self-care is essential. Many employees struggle to establish healthy professional boundaries, which can ultimately contribute to burnout due to a lack of self-care.

Not only do employees have a responsibility to take care of themselves, but employers also need to be intentional about wellness programs. I'm encouraged to see that companies and organizations are becoming more cognizant of the prevalence of burnout. A survey conducted by the American Psychological Association in 2022 provided promising results. It revealed that employer-provided support for mental health has seen a significant increase, with 71% of employees reporting that their employers now exhibit greater concern for the mental well-being of their staff.

I'm currently under a consulting contract with the Chino Police Department in Chino, California. One aspect that stands out about this department is their commitment to an Officer Wellness and Mental Health Program, a common initiative among law enforcement agencies. The Chino Police Department prioritizes this program, demonstrating a strong and healthy organizational culture. Their leadership is dedicated to mitigating stress and addressing burnout issues proactively.

A Walden University Study revealed that police officers report higher rates of depression, anxiety, post-traumatic stress disorder (PTSD), suicide, and burnout than many other professions. The same report also revealed that many police officers don't have the ability to recognize when they are experiencing burnout or mental health issues. Further, many police officers aren't likely to take the initiative to get the help and support needed, which is why wellness programs are essential. My friend, Chief Kevin Mensen, the Chief of Police for the Chino

Police Department, is serious about taking care of his officers and staff. I point to him and his department specifically because they are *intentional*. It is my hope that if you're an organizational leader, you will follow this example and begin to implement similar programs.

What Burnout Isn't

The purpose of this chapter is to help you understand and properly define burnout. I've established that burnout is real and serious. It is a growing epidemic, plaguing the workplace and the individual quality of life. Before we dive into what burnout is, I am reminded of a word of advice that I received many years ago. Someone told me that, before you can define what something is, you must first define what it is *not*.

In this next section, I want to build a fence. Within the parameters of the fence, I will identify what burnout really is. Outside the fence is what burnout is NOT. Let's work *outside* the fence first because there are so many misconceptions about burnout. People have placed labels on burnout that simply aren't true, making it difficult to properly manage burnout.

Burnout Isn't A Medical Condition

Even though burnout has physical symptoms, it is not a medical condition. For example, my burnout experience was characterized by fatigue, headaches, and insomnia; however, these characteristics do not make burnout a medical problem. Left untreated, the physical symptoms of burnout may escalate into more severe medical conditions. However, it's important to note that burnout itself is not classified as a medical issue.

Burnout has gained significant attention in recent years and is widely recognized as a serious issue affecting individuals' well-being. This has led to an ongoing debate about whether it should be classified as a medical condition. While many medical studies have been conducted on burnout, there is a lack of clear diagnostic criteria. One primary reason burnout isn't universally accepted as a medical condition is due to the absence of standardized and objective diagnostic criteria.

Medical conditions have clear biological markers, but burnout is largely defined by subjective experiences such as emotional exhaustion, depersonalization, and reduced personal accomplishment. The lack of clear, measurable parameters makes it challenging to diagnose burnout consistently across different individuals and groups.

Another factor to consider involves sociocultural and environmental influences. Burnout is often linked to workplace stress, organizational dynamics, and broader societal pressures. While these factors undoubtedly impact individuals' well-being, they are not inherently medical. Unlike medical conditions, which have objective diagnostic criteria, burnout is characterized by subjective experiences. Individual perceptions of burnout can vary widely, influenced by factors such as personal resilience, coping strategies, and cultural norms. This subjective nature of burnout raises doubts about the reliability and validity of diagnosing it as a medical condition.

Burnout Isn't a Mental Illness

Our society has done a major disservice in the treatment and recovery of burnout because of stigmatization. There are blurred boundaries between burnout and established psychiatric conditions. Burnout does share overlapping symptoms with various mental health issues, but it cannot be classified as a mental illness for the same reason that it cannot be classified as a medical condition. There are subjective and environmental factors that lead to burnout.

One way that we have labeled burnout is that it is a condition. Probably a better term would be to call it a syndrome. In the mental health field, you will not find burnout listed in the *Diagnostic and Statistical Manual of Mental Disorders*. Burnout simply doesn't have the diagnostic criteria qualifying it as a mental disorder. Mental illnesses are diagnosed based on specific criteria that consider the severity, duration, and impairment of functioning.

The proper diagnosis of burnout has to consider the origin and context. Burnout is rooted in workplace stressors, such as excessive workload, lack of control, and unclear job expectations. Mental illnesses often have multifaceted causes, including genetic, biological, environmental, and psychological factors.

Burnout Isn't the Same as Stress

Let's get this straight: while prolonged stress often leads to burnout, stress is not the same as burnout. We all live with stress every day. One essential life skill is stress management, and there are numerous approaches to achieve it. Stress can be categorized into two types: eustress and distress. Eustress, or "good stress," occurs when we feel excited, resulting in a surge of hormones without any fear or threat. This type of stress is short-term, inspiring and motivating us while enhancing performance. On the other hand, distress, or "bad stress," leads to anxiety and wears us down over time.

Stress often arises from being overly engaged, with packed calendars and overwhelming tasks. Burnout, however, is marked by disengagement. Even if you're not overworked, you feel disconnected and lack passion for your work. This phenomenon, known as "quiet quitting," is becoming increasingly prevalent across America. Many employees show up to work each day and go through the motions, but they lack enthusiasm and passion for their tasks.

There is also a difference in the way we express emotions. When we get stressed, often, we are reactive in our emotions. When couples get stressed, they argue and lash out at each other. In the workplace, when people feel stress, they express their emotions to each other in reactive and improper ways. A person going through burnout has distant emotions.

Let me shed some light on my burnout journey. Despite experiencing burnout, I managed to fulfill my job responsibilities. However, I became emotionally distant. I withdrew from interacting with the team I supervised and ceased having meaningful conversations with them. My communication with them was limited to work-related matters, confined to meetings and one-on-one discussions. Outside of these interactions, I avoided spending time with them.

In my last year working at the church as the Business Administrator, I stopped going to lunch with folks. I lived just two miles from the church and every day, without fail, I'd go home for my lunch hour. I was that checked out. I was distant and disengaged emotionally. I vividly remember sitting on my sofa, eating lunch alone, dreading going back to the office.

Now, that's burnout! Anyone who knows me knows I'm an extreme extrovert—I love being around people and being social! During my burnout, not only did I *not* want to be around people at the office, I stopped caring altogether. I had no desire to be emotionally connected to them. I saw them as employees, no longer as friends.

With stress, we experience diminished energy. With burnout, our energy is completely lost. Stress leads to anxiety, but burnout can lead to feeling depressed. I remember feeling hopeless. Not only did I experience a loss of passion and energy, but I also felt a deep sense of depression. I grew to dislike both my work and the environment in which I was working. While stress typically manifests as physical strain, burnout primarily manifests as emotional strain.

Burnout Isn't Depression

While depression can be a *part* of burnout, the two are not synonymous. Depression is a mental health disorder characterized by persistent feelings of sadness, hopelessness, and a lack of interest or pleasure in activities. Depression can be treated with medication. Medication does *not* treat burnout.

Depression involves a broad range of symptoms, including changes in appetite, sleep disturbances, feelings of guilt or worthlessness, and difficulty concentrating. It can affect various aspects of your life—not just work. Burnout is usually attributed to the (often negative) environmental factors at work. It could be the culture of the organization or team, working for a poor leader, unrealistic expectations, overload, and other organizational dynamics. For the most part, burnout is connected to our work; it's circumstantial. The path to recovery from burnout begins when we take action to change our work circumstances.

Burnout Isn't a Nervous Breakdown

Burnout typically does not escalate to a nervous breakdown, which is a serious mental health crisis often colloquially used to describe severe emotional distress. Mental health professionals do not classify it as a clinical term. A nervous breakdown entails a sudden inability to cope with stress and overwhelming emotions, resulting in impaired functioning. Individuals experiencing a nervous breakdown may lose all coping skills and struggle to function in various aspects of life, including at home, work, or in other situations.

Defining Burnout

Now that we've fenced out what burnout isn't, we can explore what burnout really is. If we do not fully understand what it is, we are led to misconceptions and a lack of knowledge of how to recover. Not understanding burnout can cause us to oversimplify the syndrome. Going back to my story, that is precisely what I did in my two-year journey. I oversimplified what I was feeling and experiencing, in part due to my pride; I didn't want to appear weak. There was also the fear factor. I couldn't bear the idea of my staff, board, and supervisor to discredit me, thus putting my job in jeopardy. I also assumed that I could just hit a switch and, one day, I would wake up, and the burnout would be gone.

Not comprehending burnout often leads to its dismissal and even stigmatization. I want to emphasize and urge you not to ignore burnout if you're experiencing symptoms. If you're a manager and notice signs of burnout in your employees, address it with them and ensure they receive the necessary support and assistance. Above all, avoid stigmatizing yourself or others experiencing burnout. Recognize that it's a condition that can be reversed.

Burnout is characterized by emotional, mental, and physical exhaustion resulting from prolonged and excessive stress. It encompasses emotional exhaustion, depersonalization, and demoralization. Burnout occurs when your internal resources are unable to cope with external demands. That's why workplace factors are often central to addressing burnout, as it's typically linked to our professional roles.

You can be physically exhausted without being emotionally exhausted. I say that to place a warning sign before you. I failed to see this initial warning sign. When I would go on vacation to address my fatigue, I always came back to work somewhat physically refreshed—but I was emotionally drained, even though I had been on a fun vacation. That's burnout!

Burnout also involves depersonalization. This means you lose your sense of identity. You get out of touch with who you are. You lose that sense of fulfillment, purpose, and passion. Your reality gets distorted, especially the way you see yourself. You begin to doubt yourself. You lose confidence in your abilities, especially your professional competence. Burnout also includes demoralization. You have feelings of helplessness, hopelessness, and meaninglessness.

In this first chapter, we've built a fence, establishing boundaries by distinguishing what burnout is and what it is not. Now, in the next chapter, we'll delve into some of the primary causes of burnout.

CHAPTER 2

CAUSES OF BURNOUT

In May of 2020, I had reached peak burnout. Two months into the COVID shutdown, most people were working from home—myself included. I mentioned earlier that my burnout started back in 2018, slowly escalating over the next year and a half. Right after the shutdown, my burnout had developed into a chronic condition.

As a marathon runner, I typically go for long runs on Saturday mornings. It's a way for me to disconnect, get some fresh air, and enjoy time with friends. That May, I was out on a 15-mile run with some running buddies. When I got back home, I had three voicemails. Two were from staff members I'd supervised; they were always arguing and butting heads. I often had to step in and serve as a mediator to help them resolve their issues. Now, these two were fighting again over something small, which was pretty typical. I spoke with each of them separately, listened to their perspectives, provided guidance, and made decisions to address the situation. While they were satisfied with the outcome, I found myself drained after each conversation. It wasn't just the trivial nature of their disagreement that left me exhausted, but rather the recurring pattern of conflict between them.

The third voicemail was from my supervisor. Because these two staff members couldn't reach me immediately, they circumvented me and contacted my supervisor about their issue. He was displeased with me for not being readily available and had to listen to their grievances about each other, a situation he didn't want to handle. I couldn't understand why I should be expected to mediate between two adults bickering over a trivial matter, on a Saturday morning no less!

After returning all three calls and resolving the issue, I still didn't feel okay. I found myself frustrated and utterly drained, plunging into an emotional whirlwind. Sitting on my sofa, I couldn't help but exclaim, "I can't handle this anymore!" Doubts about my competence and professional skills began to creep in. I reflected on my options and I asked myself, *How did I get to this level of burnout? Why am I burned out? What conditions led to this professional exhaustion?*

That day was a defining moment for me. I realized it was time to address my burnout. It was at this point I decided to take action. I composed an email to my supervisor and was very transparent about my level of burnout. While I had already shared with him my feelings of burnout, I had downplayed it. However, in this particular email, I was very honest with him, clearly stating that I needed to do something.

In the email, I presented my supervisor with three options. The first was to take early retirement. The second was to change my position and/or job description, which would include my supervisory responsibilities. The third was to take a sabbatical. We later met to discuss my burnout and the options I'd posed to him.

In regards to taking an early retirement, my supervisor believed I was too young and still had so much to give and contribute. I took that as a compliment. In my heart of hearts, I knew he was right. I was only 56 at the time; healthy and vibrant (other than the burnout, of course!). Additionally, he wasn't open at all to the idea of revising my role. So, that left only one option: a sabbatical. He didn't like that option because he felt it would leave a huge hole in the operations and functions at our church since I was the Business Administrator. Even though he didn't like it and I knew it would probably cost me my job, I needed to take some time off.

I submitted a proposal to the board, ultimately leading to my decision to take a 10-week sabbatical. While drafting the proposal, I engaged in further reflection on how I had reached the point of burnout. One key factor was my failure to address it promptly. Pride played a role; I didn't want to appear weak. Additionally, my lack of understanding and experience with burnout led me to believe I could simply snap out of it eventually. Looking back, I realize I should have confronted it and been honest about it much sooner.

In this chapter, I aim to explore some of the root causes of burnout. My hope is that you'll use this information as a guide. When you recognize these signs in your own life, I urge you to take immediate action to halt the downward spiral.

Acute vs. Chronic Burnout

Psychologists and counselors say there are two types of burnout: acute and chronic. Acute burnout refers to a sudden onset of the signs and the emotional exhaustion. As soon as you recognize the signs, it is important to stop the slide and take immediate action to address it. Chronic or "insidious" burnout is subtle, gradual, and progressive. Psychologists say this type is more difficult to resolve.

I suffered from chronic burnout because it was an 18-month slide. I didn't recognize it at first, but the signs were there. I just ignored them. Mine was also chronic because of the degree and intensity of my condition. Chronic burnout creeps up on you because you are unaware of what is going on and, the next thing you know, you either hit the wall or the wall is right in front of you. I didn't crash and burn, but I did touch the wall because I allowed its subtle nature to take over my life.

At the time of this writing, I am now four years out from my burnout experience. I have had time to reflect on why and how I went through burnout and I want to share those learnings with you. I've also spent much time researching the subject and can attest that what I've learned matches my personal experience.

I believe burnout can stem from both internal and external factors, as evidenced by my own story and experience. Internal factors relate to your individual makeup and how you're wired, which can significantly contribute to burnout. External factors, on the other hand, are related to your environment. Certain environmental conditions can foster the development of burnout.

Internal Factors of Burnout

While external factors undoubtedly influence burnout, understanding the internal contributors is equally essential for prevention, mitigation, and recovery strategies. Let's explore a few of them.

Personality Traits

The connection between personality traits and burnout is complex. Burnout, marked by emotional exhaustion, depersonalization, and reduced personal accomplishment, is increasingly prevalent in today's fast-paced world, particularly in work settings. Recognizing the influence of personality traits on burnout's development is essential for crafting effective interventions.

Burnout studies have been conducted using the association with the *Big Five Personality Traits which include* openness, conscientiousness, extraversion, agreeableness, and neuroticism. Findings from these studies suggest that individuals high in neuroticism may be more prone to burnout because of their high susceptibility to stress and negative emotions.

The word neuroticism is not only a fancy, technical word, but sounds like an illness, doesn't it? It is not a mental illness or medical condition. It is a core personality type characterized by anxiety, self-doubt, and negative feelings. Research suggests that neuroticism in personalities makes one more inclined to burnout.

These same studies reveal that individuals with high levels of conscientiousness and agreeableness are often associated with lower burnout risk, because these traits contribute to resilience and positive interpersonal relations.

Agreeableness refers to those individuals who are compassionate and cooperative, rather than antagonistic toward others. In regards to burnout, people who are intrinsically and naturally compassionate show lower levels of burnout. They demonstrate empathy and deep emotional connections with people, which causes them to be more healthy and stable relationally.

They are also cooperative. People who are antagonistic and always challenging others often find themselves frustrated and they are constantly in conflict with others. This can grow to be tiring and exhausting and can wreak havoc on your emotional well-being.

Conscientiousness is a term that describes individuals who are responsible, organized, goal-oriented, and adhere to rules and norms. There are two significant things to note here. People who are organized generally have great time management skills. Time management is crucial in today's workplace because many professionals have a myriad of tasks and responsibilities. Organization and proper time management helps professionals prevent burnout because they are able to organize and manage their work better. The implication here is chaos in schedules and responsibilities breeds the propensity for burnout. One may not be able to eliminate responsibilities on the job, but they can organize their work in such a way to reduce stress, which leads to professional burnout.

The other significant aspect of conscientiousness is the adherence to rules and norms. If an individual is always fighting systems, rules and norms, they will eventually wear out because, often, they have no control over the things they are attempting to change.

It is also important to consider the *Type A/B Model.* This model has also been examined in the discussion and context of burnout. Type A individuals are characterized by competitiveness and a sense of urgency. As a result of those traits, they may experience higher levels of burnout due to stress. Type B individuals are more laid-back and less time-pressured and exhibit lower susceptibility to burnout.

I have a Type A Personality. I have demonstrated and exhibited Type A traits all of my life. I started playing baseball when I was 8 years old and played through high school. I was very competitive. I had to be the best player on the team. I had to have the highest batting average, most stolen bases, and the highest runs batted in. Not only did I compete with others, but I competed with myself. I was always challenging and pushing myself. At times, it was miserable because, no matter how good I was, it was never quite enough.

Growing up in West Tennessee in a small rural town, I have fond memories of spending baseball off-seasons in the cold, harsh winter weather. I would take my two younger brothers to one of our crop fields on our land, where one brother would pitch to me for batting practice while the other fetched the balls. Being the oldest of three certainly had its advantages! I was driven to excel and be the best.

While this competitiveness may have been acceptable for a kid or teenager striving to compete at a high level, I unfortunately carried this behavior into adulthood. Upon reflecting on my four years of introspection, I've come to realize that this personality trait significantly contributed to my experience of burnout in my career and other aspects of life.

In my doctoral program, I had the privilege of studying under Dr. Archibald Hart, a highly respected Christian psychologist. During one of his lectures, he talked about the Type A/B Model and its association with burnout. He said that while one cannot change their personality, changes can be made to personality *behaviors*. That statement stuck with me and I still recite it. Over the years, I've tried to alter Type A behaviors that worked against me.

After going through chronic burnout and learning that my personality contributed significantly to my condition, I have worked on altering some of my behaviors.

For instance, I used to be a fast walker, driven by a constant sense of urgency and time pressure. Now, I consciously slow down to savor the moments and appreciate the people around me. I've been working hard to embrace my natural drive while ensuring it doesn't become detrimental. I can honestly say I've shifted from being a Type A personality to more of a Type A-. My former teachers might not be thrilled, as I'm now content with achieving a slightly lower grade. Go ahead, you can humor me with a laugh on that one!

Mindsets

Another internal factor is our mindset. Mindset is now a huge buzzword in today's world, and rightly so. Our mindset is important for how we function in the world. Mindset refers to an individual's beliefs and attitudes that shape their cognitive processes and how they perceive and respond to challenges.

Obviously, external factors like personal and professional challenges contribute to burnout, which we will focus on a bit later, but how we think about those challenges will determine a person's resilience and ability to cope. I teach mindset in keynote addresses and training seminars, and one of my statements is: If you want to change how you feel, you must first change how you think. Our thoughts influence our feelings and our behaviors.

Psychologist Carol Dweck is the one who first proposed the concept of fixed and growth mindsets. A fixed mindset assumes the position that abilities and intelligence are static. In other words, there is a ceiling on what you can learn and how much you can develop. A growth mindset sees abilities and intelligence as malleable through effort and learning.

Individuals with a fixed mindset may be particularly vulnerable to burnout. The belief that abilities are unchangeable can instill a fear of failure, where setbacks are interpreted as reflections of inherent deficiencies. This fear, compounded by the constant pressures of the workplace, can ultimately lead to emotional exhaustion.

Many working Americans are unhappy in their jobs. There are many reasons for this lack of satisfaction. It could be a negative workplace culture, poor leadership, heavy workload, among other factors. Sometimes employees feel powerless in changing their situation. This is where your mindset is your best resource. Ruminating on the negative aspects of your job can take you down a path of emotional exhaustion. If you can't change your situation, you have to shift your thinking about your situation. Shifting your mindset will help your attitude.

Perfectionism

Can I be honest with you? All of my life, I have struggled with perfectionism. In some ways, it has worked in my favor because I've strived for excellence and I am committed to excellence. But, in other ways, having a perfectionist mindset has worked against me. I tend to expect *so* much from life, others, and even myself. As a perfectionist, I've sabotaged many projects and relationships.

How can you know that you are a perfectionist? The perfectionist mindset helps you to be diligent and conscientious but it also leads to overthinking and second-guessing. Second-guessing can lead to making the wrong decisions because we overthink. It can also lead to not making a decision at all because we sacrifice good or excellent for perfect. Perfectionists also have unrealistic expectations that carry over into every aspect of life. When we set expectations too high, we often find ourselves disappointed in ourselves. The perfectionist mindset also places pressure on the people in our lives. Because we set the standards too high, others often feel that they cannot measure up to our expectations, so we push them away. I have found this, all too often, to be true in my life. If you are a perfectionist, then you are probably a control freak. A perfectionist is highly structured and organized, but we have to be careful about getting caught up in control issues.

Perfectionism leads to burnout because trying to make everything perfect is tiring and draining. Nothing is ever good enough for perfectionists. We are never satisfied with ourselves. We often find ourselves disappointed in people. We have a hard time celebrating progress because we hyper-fixate on that one thing we could've—and should've—done better. Perfectionism can be a miserable place to live.

Perfectionists are often control freaks. We don't live in a perfect world and most things are not perfect in our individual lives. Let's face it, we have very little control over most things. The strain and toil of trying to make everything perfect takes its toll and can eventually lead to burnout.

Luckily, I have some great news for you! If you are like me and struggle with perfectionism, you need to understand that you can make changes. Neurologists use the term *plasticity* to describe the functionality of the human brain. The brain can create new neural networks, which gives the brain the capacity to change with learning. Our tendencies and behaviors can be changed by rewiring and retraining our brain.

You are probably thinking, "Now, Reggie, enough of this technical neurological stuff... just tell me, how can I rewire my brain if I'm a perfectionist?" Well, I'm so glad you asked. Here's some advice for you:

- Learn to LOVE your imperfect self. Accept the reality that neither you nor anyone else is perfect. No one else expects perfection from you and neither should you. Practice self-compassion and learn to give yourself grace.
- Set realistic expectations for yourself and others. Get to know yourself. Identify your strengths and growth areas. You cannot be good at everything; learn to be content with excellence and don't chase perfection. You will never achieve it and you will find yourself constantly being frustrated and disappointed with yourself. Adopt this same mindset in your relationships, whether it is with your marriage, kids, friends, co-workers, or bosses. Set high expectations, but not *unrealistic* expectations.
- Give yourself permission to fail. To do this, you have to change your mindset or way of thinking. Adopt a growth mindset. Remember, the growth mindset is the belief that we are always learning and growing. Often, those lessons come from failure. *Failure is NOT the opposite of success; it is a part of success.*

Success often comes from the lessons learned through our failures.

- Focus on your character, not just your accomplishments. Perfectionists are task-oriented. Our identity is tied to our accomplishments. If we feel accomplished and successful, then we feel good about ourselves. If we feel we are not accomplishing and at a certain level, this diminishes our images of ourselves. Focus on WHO you are; not WHAT you do!
- Enjoy the process; not just the outcome. Perfectionists are often impatient, always eager to see the results and outcomes. Embrace every step that you take as you're working on a project or task and celebrate as you make progress.

Just because you're a perfectionist doesn't mean you're destined to burnout. Psychologists tell us there is maladaptive perfectionism and adaptive perfectionism. It is important to understand the difference between the two types.

Maladaptive perfectionism is unhealthy. Individuals with this type believe they can control their environment and achieve their unrealistic standards all the time. They tend to be aggressive with others, highly self-critical, and prone to anxiety, stress, depression, and, yes, burnout!

Adaptive perfectionism is the healthy type. Individuals with this type also strive for personal standards and achievements, but are much more realistic about it. These individuals set goals and strive for the accomplishment of them, but they do not beat themselves up when they do not achieve them. In fact, they are not only more realistic, but more resilient. If plan A doesn't work, they work on plan B. I always tell people that if plan A doesn't work, there are 25 more letters in the alphabet! People with adaptive perfectionism also have the ability to be satisfied with their efforts and progress, even when the desired standards are not met.

External Factors of Burnout

One of the reasons for burnout being so pervasive is that many professionals have inadequate coping mechanisms. Without the proper coping skills, we can hit the dreaded wall of emotional exhaustion. We have talked about some internal factors that lead to burnout, so let's consider the *external* factors, also known as environmental factors.

Heavy Workload

In a 2010 report, BMC Public Health identified three types of employee burnout: frenetic, under-challenged, and worn-out. Frenetic burnout impacts individuals who overwork themselves to the point of exhaustion. They go above and beyond to achieve their goals and view their work ethic as a point of pride, even though it can negatively impact their lives and well-being.

Overworking is a significant contributor to burnout, a challenge encountered by many employees at some stage. While certain periods in our jobs, professions, and careers may demand more from us, it's crucial to recognize that this pace is only sustainable for short durations. One study found that 95% of employees experience external pressure to overwork.

Numerous factors contribute to heavy workloads, such as demanding bosses, ineffective management practices, staffing shortages, treating everything as a top priority, unrealistic expectations, disorganization, and inefficient systems, among others. These heavy workloads generate unhealthy levels of stress, a trend that seems to be increasingly common, contributing to the current epidemic of burnout.

Inc and Go recently conducted a survey of over 1,000 employees, with a particular focus on the prevalence of overworking culture. The study aimed to understand the frequency of overtime work and its effects. The findings revealed that 71% of respondents worked overtime at least once a week, with 30% working 2-3 times a week, and 19% working overtime nearly every day of the week.

There is what I call a "culture of overworking." This type of culture is created by leaders who generally don't care about their employees and their well-being. All they care about is the actual work, without regards to how their employees are doing. Overworking has become an unspoken expectation and is often glorified, which I find troubling. This culture deprives employees of a balanced quality of life and ultimately results in worn-out and disengaged employees.

One of my biggest frustrations is hearing employees boast about never taking vacations, working weekends, bringing work home, and sacrificing quality family time. They wear overworking as a badge of honor, but it's detrimental to their well-being. To stay engaged and productive, employees need to disconnect to recharge emotionally. Celebrating overwork and embracing such a lifestyle isn't just unhealthy—it's foolish.

Work-Life Imbalance

You may have heard of the four C's that diamond jewelers often discuss when selling a diamond ring to a customer. These include cut, color, clarity, and carat weight. *Have you ever wondered why some diamonds sparkle more than others?* It has to do with the cut. The more cuts a diamond has, the more it sparkles. The same is true of our lives. We need many facets of our lives to truly enjoy life. We cannot be one-dimensional. Our lives have to be more than just about our work. It's essential to strike a balance in our lives, ensuring we spend quality time with family, connect with friends, pursue hobbies and recreational activities, and enjoy all the other aspects of life.

The inability to strike a balance between professional and personal commitments can lead to burnout. An overwhelming focus on work at the expense of personal life will result in fatigue and a diminished sense of well-being.

Under-challenged Burnout

We often associate burnout with overworking, pressing deadlines, and unrealistic expectations. The constant pressure of being challenged and overloaded definitely contributes to burnout. Did you know that the opposite is also true? Being under-challenged is also a contributing factor to burnout. Research shows that boredom and monotony cause emotional exhaustion. Sounds a bit odd, doesn't it?

My dad spent many years working in an aluminum plant. During a couple of summers while I was in college, I worked alongside him at the plant to earn money for tuition. Observing my dad and the other workers in the plant, I noticed they went through the same routine every day—operating the same machines, pressing the same buttons, and producing the same product. While I admired my dad for being a reliable provider, I couldn't imagine doing that repetitive work for over 20 years.

I am not wired like my dad. Over the course of my 30 years as a working professional, I have changed jobs many times. I get bored easily. After I am on a job for a while, it becomes routine and somewhat boring, because I feel there is nothing else to learn. I mentally disengage and find myself in need of a new challenge. I don't like monotony. I like to be challenged.

One of my running friends, Jim Powell, has worked as a civil engineer for over 30 years. Not only that, but he has worked for the same company for many of those years. I admire Jim for his loyalty, passion and consistency, but I know I would go nuts doing the same job at the same company for that long. Under-challenged burnout is typified by a loss of purpose or disengagement from work. These workers find their jobs under stimulating due to general dissatisfaction.

Referring back to my story, chronic burnout stemmed from a combination of internal and external factors. As mentioned earlier, one contributing factor was feeling bored, disengaged, and under-stimulated. After three decades in ministry and the repetitive nature of my role as the Business Administrator in the church had become monotonous. It felt akin to working in an aluminum plant for decades—repeating the same tasks day in and day out, merely going through the motions.

Was I good at my job? Yes. Was I competent? Yes. Was I fulfilled? Nope! The Maslach Burnout Inventory (MBI) deals with three dimensions of burnout including emotional exhaustion, depersonalization, and reduced personal accomplishment.

We've already established that burnout includes emotional exhaustion. That means there are overwhelming feelings of depletion of emotional resources and the inability to cope with the demands of the job. During my 18-month burnout journey, I experienced a gradual buildup of emotional exhaustion, although initially, I didn't recognize it as burnout. As I approached the metaphorical wall and felt myself nearing a breaking point, I reached a stage where I simply lacked the energy to carry on. It became evident that I needed to take a break.

Depersonalization is cynicism. Burnout is also characterized by a negative and detached attitude towards one's work, colleagues, and the recipients under your care. Boy, was I there, especially around the time of the COVID shutdown. I didn't always show negativity toward my staff and colleagues, but I sure felt it. I became emotionally detached from the job itself and the people with whom I worked.

Then there is reduced personal accomplishment. According to Maslach, this is a decline in feelings of competence and successful achievement in one's work. I had lost that. I lost my passion for my work. I didn't feel competent or successful because I had a negative view of myself. Depersonalization could also be called emotional demoralization. In my case, I felt this because I was bored, felt stuck, and felt that I was no longer learning and growing.

CHAPTER 3

MANAGING JOB BURNOUT

Chuck Thompson is not just a close friend; he's one of my best friends whom I've known for many years. Hailing from Virginia, Chuck and I share a deep bond as both close personal companions and fellow marathon enthusiasts. We've logged countless miles and tackled numerous races side by side, relishing each other's company along the way. Chuck embodies the essence of friendship—he supports me unconditionally and holds me accountable, encouraging me to strive for the best version of myself.

Chuck attended a military college with the hopes of studying computer science; he loved technology. He was ahead of his time in terms of his technological knowledge and skills. Even though that was his dream profession, he ultimately decided to go into engineering because of his dad who worked as an engineering assistant.

Chuck didn't choose his profession out of a desire to follow in his father's footsteps; rather, it was his father's insistence that he pursue engineering. Wanting to avoid conflict with his father and trusting his opinion, Chuck opted for this path.

When he entered college, Chuck initially pursued electrical engineering. However, realizing it wasn't the right fit for him, he made the decision to switch to civil engineering. Graduating with this major, he embarked on a successful career in the field.

Chuck accumulated a wealth of experience over the course of his career, spanning various sectors. He dedicated 8 years to a county agency, followed by 2 ½ years in a city position. Subsequently, he spent 5 years in a private firm before venturing out to establish his own successful firm, where he thrived for another 5 years.

Following his tenure in the industry, Chuck transitioned to a part-time role as the Building & Grounds Manager at the church where I served as Business Administrator, dedicating 5 years to this role. Seeking greater fulfillment and freedom, he eventually resigned to pursue his passions. Today, Chuck finds joy and fulfillment as a Running

Coach, embracing a career path that resonates deeply with him.

Chuck's story serves as a valuable example, highlighting a common cause of burnout discussed in Chapter 2: being under-challenged. While he may question whether he truly experienced burnout, his experience aligns with this phenomenon.

Chuck's personality thrives on growth and learning. When faced with stagnant environments devoid of challenge, he quickly becomes disengaged and bored. This led him to switch jobs regularly throughout his career, even within the same organization, as he sought to maintain a sense of freshness and avoid monotony.

After moving into a new division at his county position, his first performance review was quite alarming. Chuck is a highly responsible and competent person and always received "outstanding" ratings in his reviews. However, when he had his first review, his supervisor rated him only "competent." Under this supervisor's policy, newcomers to the division were limited to receiving a "competent" rating, positioned at the midpoint of the rating scale.. Even though Chuck had a lot of experience and was extremely good at his craft, his supervisor still rated him lower than what Chuck really deserved. Naturally, this policy bothered Chuck, as it seemed unfair and limiting. This, along with other cultural issues within the organization, troubled him.

Chuck shared with me that when he went to meetings and looked around at some of his colleagues he thought, I don't want to become like them. He saw colleagues who were unhealthy because they did not practice self-care. The work-life balance in his agency was tough to manage. In fact, Chuck worked 70-80 hours a week and he was falling into some unhealthy patterns.

This was a wake-up call for him. He found himself overweight and out of balance. He was working long hours, not spending enough time with his family, and missing a number of his kids' activities. He grew tired of that. Besides, he no longer found being an engineer satisfying and energizing.

Physically, Chuck was unhappy with his condition, weighing in at 252 pounds and dealing with gastrointestinal issues likely exacerbated by job stress. Emotionally, he felt drained and disconnected. Despite his initiative and commitment to dependability, he found himself engaging in what he termed "disengaged engagement" – completing tasks mechanically without passion or fulfillment. For Chuck, engineering had become merely a means to an end.

Today, I'm happy to say that Chuck is very happy and has great balance in his life. With an ability to focus on spending more time with his family, he's enjoying the freedom that comes with having more control over his life. He is now living life with a newfound passion, zest, and enthusiasm. I asked him what advice he would give to professionals who are feeling what he felt.

"Pursue what you can do to be successful and do something that will help you achieve your overall life goals," he said. You see, even as a teenager and young adult, Chuck's primary goal in life was to build a happy, healthy, and functional family. Chuck has a wonderful family and has achieved that goal, but feels that it was a strain and challenge because his chosen career did not support achieving that goal. Put another way, the nature and responsibility of his position did not naturally fit what he wanted to accomplish for his life.

I want to clarify that I'm not suggesting that if you're experiencing burnout or recovering from it, you need to abandon your career or job entirely. Chuck's story is specific to him. Instead, we need to find ways to effectively manage burnout in the workplace. In this chapter, we'll delve into some strategies to help you do just that.

Burnout's Effect on the Workplace

In my day-to-day life, I have many conversations about burnout. In my consultations with organizational leaders, many have shared concerns about various issues within their organizations. These include disengaged employees, increased sick leave, challenges with retaining talented staff, decreased productivity, lack of initiative, and overall poor performance. *Could these issues be linked to burnout?* I strongly believe so. I also talk to employees who tell me they're tired, stressed out, and no longer passionate about their jobs. Many workers are struggling—it's evident that burnout is increasingly common in the modern workplace.

There is a clear connection between employee engagement and workplace burnout, according to research by Gallup. Burned-out employees are 13% less confident in their work performance. This is the aspect of burnout called *depersonalization.* Depersonalization is the development of a negative and detached attitude about one's work. It leads to disengagement and a lack of motivation. Disengagement is the fruit; the root is depersonalization and this happens when employees feel less competent within themselves. The attitude about themselves manifests itself in the outward fruit of low morale, low productivity, and low engagement. Let's consider some other statistics:

- Burned-out employees are significantly more likely to actively seek new job opportunities, with research showing a 2.6 times higher likelihood compared to their non-burned-out counterparts. Moreover, a recent survey conducted by Westfield Health revealed that 59% of employees consider their mental health a primary motivation for pursuing a new role.
- Further emphasizing the impact of burnout on turnover, a study exploring the link between occupational stress, burnout, and turnover intention found that both a lack of job satisfaction and emotional exhaustion are robust predictors of employees intending to leave their current positions.
- In terms of financial repercussions, a joint report by Gallup and Workhuman uncovered that employee burnout contributes to turnover and lost productivity, resulting in an estimated cost of approximately $322 billion to businesses globally.
- According to a Chartered Institute of Personnel and Development survey, 79% of the respondents identified stress-related absences in their organization over the previous year. The number was actually higher for large organizations at 90%. Another study reported

that 17 million working days were lost to stress in 2019-2020. Burned-out U.S. workers are 63% more likely to take a sick day than happy, engaged employees, according to Gallup.

- A study conducted by the American Psychological Association found that 81% of employees will seek out workplaces that support mental health when exploring future roles, highlighting the importance of mental health benefits on employee retention.

Culture and Burnout

One's work culture can certainly contribute to burnout. Culture in the workplace encompasses the environment in which we operate, shaping our experiences and impacting our emotional well-being. A healthy organizational culture fosters positivity and productivity, while a dysfunctional one can lead to emotional exhaustion and strain.

Technically defined, culture comprises the values, beliefs, attitudes, systems, and rules that dictate and influence employee behavior within an organization. It serves as the backdrop against which employees, customers, vendors, and stakeholders interact with the organization. When discussing culture with organizational leaders and employees, I often simplify the conversation by asking, "What's it like working here?" This prompts individuals to reflect on their experiences within their workplace, whether they find fulfillment, camaraderie, and engagement, or encounter dissatisfaction and disconnection. Essentially, culture shapes morale and is inextricably linked to it.

In early 2021, a notable phenomenon emerged, dubbed the Great Resignation or the Big Quit. This trend marked a significant economic shift in the United States, as millions of individuals voluntarily chose to resign from their jobs. This trend coincided with the gradual recovery from the COVID-19 pandemic, prompting many employees to reassess their job satisfaction and overall happiness in the workplace.

I like to refer to this period as one of "Great Reflection." People had plenty of time to really reflect on their lives and not only realized that they weren't satisfied, but they wanted to make a change. Initially, many Americans attributed this trend to a desire for better pay and benefits among employees. While this may have been a factor for some individuals, it was not the primary reason behind the Great Resignation. Instead, the underlying cause was widespread dissatisfaction with work environments. Many people reached a tipping point and chose to leave their jobs in search of greater fulfillment and a healthier workplace culture.

The remainder of this chapter is for those of you who are leaders, managers, and supervisors in your organization. Earlier, I mentioned stopping the slide, and I directed that statement to those of you who are experiencing burnout. You have to take steps and measures to reverse burnout and recover from it. What I am talking about now is slowing, and even stopping, the burnout trend in your organization.

As a leader, you are the curator of culture. It is your job to set, maintain, and protect the culture of your organization. This starts with values. Values are principles or standards that reflect what is most important to you. Leaders must espouse, model, expect, and reinforce values that will create a healthy workplace culture. Certainly, there are numerous values that could be discussed, but I'm going to focus on six key ones.

1. *Empathy*

Empathy stands out as a crucial soft skill in leadership. Employees seek assurance that their leaders genuinely care about their well-being and success. William Schutz, in his book "The Human Element," identifies three fundamental psychological needs that must be addressed in the workplace to foster a healthy culture: inclusion, control, and affection. These needs, often referred to as "psychic pay," are as essential as financial compensation. When employees feel neglected in these areas, they may become resentful, disengaged, or both. Prolonged exposure to such conditions can ultimately lead to burnout.

Inclusion means employees feel a sense of belonging. Belonging within a community is a basic need of every human being and, yes, your workplace is one form of community. As human beings, our inherent need for connection and belonging is undeniable. We thrive when we feel a sense of community and belonging. However, despite being surrounded by colleagues in the workplace, individuals can still experience isolation and a lack of belonging. This feeling of disconnect can gradually lead to burnout. Therefore, as a leader, it's crucial to prioritize inclusivity and foster a sense of belonging among all employees.

Control in the workplace entails employees feeling that their work is truly valued and contributes meaningfully to the organization's mission and vision. It also encompasses a sense of competence and accomplishment. Reduced personal accomplishment, a dimension of burnout, reflects a decline in feelings of competence and achievement. Employees desire to feel competent and successful, and when this need for control is unmet, they may start to perceive themselves negatively. This can result in emotional demoralization and eventual burnout.

There is one more thing I'd like to mention about control. People enjoy having a sense of autonomy. Lack of autonomy in the workplace, including not having control over aspects like schedule, assignments, or workload, can contribute to job burnout. Research indicates that employees who work under micromanagers are more prone to burnout compared to those who have a greater sense of autonomy and control over their work.

Affection in the workplace entails employees feeling a sense of compassion and care from their leaders. It involves fostering relatedness, which is vital for psychological well-being and intrinsic motivation. Empathy plays a crucial role here, as it enables leaders to understand and share the feelings of their employees. When leaders demonstrate empathy, it fosters a sense of being cared for among employees, motivating and inspiring them. Conversely, a lack of affection in the workplace can demotivate employees and drain them of energy.

2. Appreciation and Rewards

All of us have a need to feel appreciated for the work that we do. Poor leaders often feel that all employees need to succeed at their jobs is adequate compensation. Your employees need more than that; they want to feel appreciated and *valued* for their contributions.

It is also important to reward your employees. As human beings, we can be intrinsically motivated or extrinsically motivated. Intrinsic motivation comes from within. I have to admit that I worked for a few bosses who valued showing appreciation, giving kudos or giving "that a boys/girls." Honestly, I did not look for that because I am *intrinsically* motivated. I get motivated internally by setting my own goals and achieving those goals. I am motivated by finishing a task and doing it well. Being part of the boomer generation, I've observed that our generation is inherently inclined to work hard and strive for success, driven by intrinsic motivations rather than external factors.

Unfortunately, not all employees are wired like me, driven by intrinsic motivations. Some are externally motivated, finding inspiration in tangible rewards like raises, bonuses, or praise. Regardless of their motivation style, it's crucial as a leader to provide recognition and appreciation to all employees.

As a relational leader, understanding what motivates each employee is key. By spending time with them and actively listening, you can uncover what drives them individually.

Why is this important? Because when it comes to motivation, there are only two paths: one that inspires and one that drains. Feeling appreciated fills an employee's motivation tank, while a lack of recognition can deplete it. If employees go too long without their motivation tank being refilled, they may find themselves in burnout, lacking the emotional fuel to sustain their work with enthusiasm. This not only affects their performance but also strains their emotional well-being.

3. Growth

I absolutely love working with companies that place high value on learning. Professional development is crucial in order to cultivate a healthy workplace culture. Providing opportunities that will foster growth in your employees will help your company to assemble a team that is more productive and engaged. They will constantly improve their knowledge and skills, which ultimately benefits your company.

Opportunities to learn and grow also help the employee by building their confidence, improving job satisfaction, mental health, and giving them a high level of competence. This builds their psychological and emotional stamina. Returning to my friend Chuck's story, one of the reasons he lost passion in his career is his constant need for growth and learning. When you're continuously learning and evolving, you're less likely to feel the urge to change positions or companies frequently. Staying engaged in the same role for years becomes feasible when you have opportunities to hone your skills and expand your knowledge within the organization.

Leaders who prioritize growth also welcome mistakes and failures as part of the learning process. In organizations where mistakes are penalized, creativity is stifled, and employees feel reluctant to think innovatively or suggest new ideas. However, when mistakes are viewed as valuable learning opportunities, employees are empowered to take risks and think outside the box. Embracing mistakes and failures fosters a culture of innovation and continuous improvement, ultimately leading to greater success.

4. Well-being

To avoid burnout, it's essential to replenish your physical and emotional energy through practices like maintaining good sleep habits, prioritizing nutrition, engaging in regular exercise, fostering social connections, and incorporating well-being-promoting activities into your routine. While it is the responsibility of employees to prioritize their own personal well-being, organizations need to be supportive of it. I've known many people who value well-being and a healthy work-life balance, but felt that it was in contradiction with the value system of the organization in which they worked. Their organization glorified unhealthy behaviors such as excessive workloads, working from home in the evenings, sacrificing weekends, responding to emails and calls during vacations, and other unsustainable expectations.

I do see an improving trend where organizations are really beginning to value well-being. Perhaps part of this shift is due to millennials entering the workplace and assuming leadership roles. As they now constitute nearly 50% of the workforce, they are introducing fresh values and perspectives into the workplace culture.

Millennials value professional development, autonomy, positive workplace culture, empathetic leadership, workplace flexibility, and work-life balance. For those of you who are in the boomer and Gen X generations, you may not like what I'm about to say. Frankly, millennials are not going to tolerate what other generations tolerated. They are changing the norms and values of the workplace and I find it quite refreshing.

Statistics suggest that we are making progress in the right direction. A 2022 survey conducted by the American Psychological Association, which focused on work and well-being, revealed an increase in employer-provided support for mental health. In fact, 71% of employees reported that their employers are now more concerned about the mental health of their workforce. However, it's worth noting that only

31% of respondents believed that mental health and safety initiatives had improved following the COVID-19 pandemic. In that same survey, respondents identified the most popular offers of how employers can support employees well being:

- Flexible working hours (41%)
- Workplace culture that respects time off (34%)
- The ability to work remotely (33%)
- Four-day work week (31%)
- Flexible work schedules with remote work options (a whopping 95%)

The findings from various reports offer both encouraging and concerning insights.

- According to McKinsey, a significant majority (80%) of employees believe their managers have been proactive in safeguarding the health and well-being of their teams.
- However, research by Mental Health America and FlexJobs indicates that only one in five workers feel comfortable having open and productive conversations with Human Resources about solutions to their burnout.
- Furthermore, 56% of respondents stated that their Human Resources departments do not actively encourage discussions about burnout.

While companies are implementing well-being programs, some employees may feel hesitant to admit their need for support due to a lack of psychological safety. In such cases, the onus falls on the employee to take advantage of available resources. As the saying goes, "You can lead a horse to water, but you can't make it drink." If you're experiencing burnout and your company offers support programs, it's important to utilize them. Taking advantage of these resources can help halt the progression of burnout and promote well-being.

5. *Empowerment*

My experience with burnout stemmed from a variety of factors, both internal and external. One significant external factor was my direct supervisor's micromanagement style. Upon being hired as the Business Administrator at the church, my boss assured me of the freedom and authority to support him and the organization, stating, "I'm giving you all of the keys." However, it soon became apparent that this promise would not be upheld.

One of my roles was managing and giving direction to the staff. Often, I'd help the staff set strategies and make decisions and he would override them. This also undermined my authority and credibility. It wasn't long until the staff would bypass me and go straight to him. He seemed to have enjoyed that, and I began to wonder, *why am I even here?*

My boss's micromanagement extended to questioning every decision I made regarding programs, budgets, and staff. His inquiries often delved into irrelevant details, and when I presented written documents outlining programs and budgets, he would meticulously mark them up, akin to a professor critiquing an academic paper. His need for involvement extended to every aspect of the organization's operations.

I agree that, while I might not be the smartest person in the room, I am still a pretty smart guy. In this case, I had a lot more business acumen than he had, so why didn't he just let me do my job? I've analyzed that relationship many times since leaving that position years ago. *Was he insecure? Did he not trust me?* I don't know the answer to why he micromanaged me. All I know is it was exhausting.

In 2018, about the time I started feeling burnout, I gave up. I still showed up to work and was diligent. I just didn't make decisions or create anything. I took everything to my supervisor because I knew he was going to do it his way anyway, so why waste my time? I felt like an overpaid assistant rather than a Business Administrator. At that point, I found myself simply going through the motions and carrying out his wishes after having conversations about what he wanted. Not only was I mentally and emotionally exhausted from this working relationship, I felt demoralized. I had more experience than he had, more education, and more business knowledge—but I didn't have the freedom to use my skills and talents for the good of the church. This situation accelerated my burnout trajectory.

The absence of control is indeed a significant contributor to burnout. It entails feeling powerless and having restricted authority over one's work environment, ultimately fostering a sense of helplessness that can fuel burnout.

6. Respect

Organizational leaders need to create and curate workplace cultures that are open to the needs, interests, and feelings of others. The culture of respect fosters an environment characterized by transparent communication, inclusivity, and collaboration. It values each member as a valuable thought partner and decision-maker, promoting curiosity and openness to diverse ideas.

A respectful workplace culture is one where all employees are treated fairly, differences are acknowledged and valued, communication is open and civil, conflict is addressed early and there is cooperation. Many individuals who participated in the Great Resignation cite two primary reasons for leaving their jobs: toxic workplace culture and ineffective leadership.

I want to close this chapter with some practical advice. You may have a propensity for burnout because of some internal factors like personality and mindset, but your environment plays a huge role in burnout. If you're currently seeking a position, make sure you ask more questions in your interviews than being asked of you. Ask questions about the culture, organizational values, but more important, ask the person conducting the interviews to give you examples of how they are being lived out in the organization.

Ask questions about the leadership styles of the senior leadership team because they are the ones responsible for setting the culture. If the culture and leadership dynamics do not fit you and what you are looking for, I urge you to run—run as fast as you can! If you don't, you will later regret your decision to work in those environments.

I made a huge mistake when I was interviewing for the Business Administrator position. I didn't ask about culture or leadership. The church culture was healthy, but the staff culture was dysfunctional. The senior leader's style did not fit who I was so we were misaligned.

If you find yourself in a toxic or unhealthy work culture with poor leadership, and you have the opportunity to influence change, it's worth trying to make positive adjustments. This is important because in such environments, it's often the most capable and values-driven employees who choose to leave. Their departure can further deteriorate the culture as those who remain may not have the same commitment to improving it. Therefore, if you have the ability to initiate positive changes, it can help prevent further erosion of the culture and create a better environment for everyone.

If you lack the influence, power, and authority to instigate positive cultural changes in your current organization, it may be time to seek opportunities elsewhere. Look for a workplace that aligns more closely with your core values and prioritizes employee well-being, as well as other values that are important to you.

I understand that many of you reading this book may currently find yourselves in such challenging work environments. It's important to acknowledge that financial commitments, such as mortgage payments, college tuition, and bills, can create significant concerns when considering a job change. However, it's also crucial to prioritize your emotional health and well-being alongside these financial considerations.

I hope my journey and experience can offer you some encouragement. Following my 10-week sabbatical, I found myself unexpectedly terminated from my position. Despite my proficiency in my role, the senior leader and board provided no explanation for their decision. Reflecting on the situation, I believe it was primarily due to a lack of empathy and understanding regarding my burnout.

In the upcoming chapters, I'll delve deeper into these events, providing additional insights. Looking back, however, I now see my termination as a blessing in disguise. It liberated me from an unhealthy environment. Since then, I've experienced improvements in my sleep, no longer rely on blood pressure medication, and feel more content and fulfilled professionally than ever before.

They say rejection can lead to redirection, and that's exactly what happened for me. Following my termination, I launched my own successful business aligned with my passions. Burnout didn't defeat me; it refined me.

CHAPTER 4

THE SYMPTOMS OF BURNOUT

In the journey through understanding burnout, sometimes the most illuminating stories come from those we least expect. Dr. Sean Gateley, a highly accomplished physical therapist specializing in athlete care, seemed to have it all. With a doctorate in Physical Therapy and a career path that ascended to the heights of directorship, Sean epitomized success in his field. Yet, beneath the surface of his achievements lay a hidden struggle with chronic burnout.

During his tenure at a medium-sized rehabilitation hospital, Sean's relentless ambition propelled him to remarkable heights. From his early days as a new graduate physical therapist to eventually overseeing multimillion-dollar outpatient clinics as Director of Rehabilitation and Director of Sports Medicine, Sean was the epitome of dedication. However, his ascent came at a cost.

Despite his professional triumphs, Sean's relentless workload and personal commitments began to take a toll. Working tirelessly, often seeing double the patients of his colleagues, and balancing teaching responsibilities with a growing family, Sean found himself stretched thin. What appeared to be a life brimming with success was, in reality, a facade masking the onset of burnout.

Even though he was highly productive, Sean found himself going to weekly meetings, only to be pressured by his boss to produce *more*. Sean found himself thrust into a challenging situation upon assuming the role of clinic director. Unbeknownst to him, his predecessor had left behind a financial quagmire that demanded immediate attention. As a seasoned Physical Therapist, Sean was adept at treating patients, but he lacked the business acumen required to navigate the clinic's financial woes.

Under mounting pressure from the CEO, Sean grappled with the daunting task of assuming leadership and managerial responsibilities. Despite his earnest efforts, he felt isolated and unsupported in his role. The hospital's culture, notorious for its tendency to burn out employees rather than provide the necessary training and support, only exacerbated Sean's predicament.

Seeking assistance from Human Resources, Sean's hopes for guidance were dashed when he discovered that essential training materials were withheld from him. Left to fend for himself without the requisite tools or support, Sean found himself quickly overwhelmed, both physically and emotionally.

Over time, Sean's physical and emotional distress began to manifest in alarming symptoms. He experienced chest pains—including tightness in his chest—and persistent fatigue. One day, the severity of his condition prompted him to seek urgent medical attention. Rushed to the emergency room, he was immediately admitted with a heart rate of 180 and a blood pressure of 210/110, all while experiencing atrial fibrillation.

For the next five days, Sean remained hospitalized, undergoing treatment that included blood thinners, intravenous fluids, and medications to regulate his blood pressure and heart rhythm. Recognizing the gravity of his situation, Sean was subsequently placed on medical disability for a period of three months, allowing him the necessary time to recuperate and address his health issues.

Sean had plenty of time during his leave of absence to reflect on the past couple of years he'd had. He wasn't sleeping, he was abusing caffeine, chewing tobacco, and binge drinking on his days off. He was a wreck as he slowly killed himself for a company that would replace him the second he died. Sean returned back to work after three months in a reduced capacity. He gave up his position as Director of Rehabilitation and returned to the main hospital as a staff Physical Therapist. He demanded to keep his title as Director of Sports Medicine because of all the hard work he had done to develop that program. He spent the next two years miserable and became a disgruntled employee. He was cynical, negative, and resentful. He knew he had to make a change.

In the midst of his burnout journey, Sean began exploring the possibility of opening his own clinic with some friends. As time progressed, they actively pursued this idea and eventually secured a location, leading to the establishment of Podium Sports Performance. Despite maintaining his full-time position at the hospital, Sean dedicated considerable time and effort to building the new clinic. He juggled seeing clients at Podium before and after his hospital shifts, often extending his work hours into weekends to accelerate the clinic's growth.

Through perseverance and unwavering commitment, Sean gradually expanded Podium's client base and revenue streams. This endeavor demanded significant prayer and a profound leap of faith from

Sean and his family, as they made the daunting decision to depart from his stable six-figure income at the hospital and venture into entrepreneurship.

I asked Sean what it was like continuing to work after realizing that he was in burnout. He said he felt helpless and trapped. He made good money and had great benefits, but he had to drag himself out of bed every day. He hated Mondays and couldn't wait until Friday evenings at 6:00 PM. He continued to work hard because that is who he is. There were days he wanted to call in sick, but he refused to because his colleagues and patients depended on him. Now, he was left with a serious heart condition, which he is still dealing with today. Plus, he had damaged his marriage and relationships with his friends.

Sean's confidence waned, and he grappled with feelings of failure. The once-enjoyable act of exercising lost its appeal as energy eluded him. Depressed and emotionally drained, he leaned heavily on his wife to shoulder the family's emotional burdens. Despite having a supportive circle of friends, relationships became superficial, revolving around alcohol and social gatherings. During lunch breaks, he sought solace in his car, lacking the energy to engage with colleagues.

Sean's journey epitomizes the classic trajectory of burnout, yet it also embodies hope. His path to recovery began with breaking away from the corporate world and establishing Podium Sports Performance. Today, as his own boss, supported by friends he deeply respects, Sean not only manages a thriving business but also enjoys restored health.

Through Sean's narrative, we witness the telltale signs and symptoms of burnout. Recognizing indicators such as physical and emotional exhaustion, detachment, diminished performance, and heightened cynicism is crucial for early intervention. In this chapter, we delve into these classic symptoms of burnout, urging readers to remain vigilant and proactive in addressing them to halt the downward spiral and pave the way for recovery.

Physical Symptoms

Physical exhaustion stands as a prominent physical manifestation of burnout. While fatigue after a demanding day or week at work is normal, burnout-related exhaustion runs deeper and proves more challenging to overcome. Although long hours or strenuous tasks may contribute, burnout stems from unmanaged stress and its toll on the body.

In his book "The Hidden Link Between Adrenaline and Stress," Dr. Archibald Hart offers valuable insights into this phenomenon. Burnout occurs when stress levels remain consistently high, surpassing our ability to alleviate them.

Stress is a part of normal everyday life. In fact, we need a certain amount of stress in our lives to function and stay alive. We cannot aim to live completely stress-free, but we can manage our stress so that it is healthy and helpful in being effective in our responsibilities. Stress is often thought of as tension or anxiety, but Dr. Hart's book emphasizes living in a state of *overstress*.

Dr. Hart's book delves into the detrimental impact of stress on our physical and emotional well-being. He emphasizes how the adrenal glands release adrenaline to aid us in fight or flight situations, but after such responses, our bodies must return to a state of low arousal. Sustained high arousal is unsustainable.

Two mechanisms underlie anxiety. Firstly, the brain's receptors receive hormones, prompting the production of natural tranquilizers in response to stress. However, prolonged stress can deplete this supply. Secondly, cortisol, a stress hormone, inhibits the brain's natural tranquilizers, escalating anxiety levels and potentially leading to panic or anxiety attacks.

Notably, Dr. Hart distinguishes between good and bad stress, highlighting that even positive events and essential responsibilities can induce harmful stress. Additionally, the book underscores the existence of hidden stressors, wherein our bodies experience distress without our conscious awareness, underscoring the potential for subtle yet impactful stressors to affect us.

Understanding the body's adrenaline arousal and its defense systems is crucial for managing stress. These defense systems include the alarm system, activating system, and recovery system. The alarm system alerts us when our bodies are pushed to their limits, while the activating system boosts our strength and alertness to respond effectively. Conversely, the recovery system aims to facilitate healing and recuperation.

Dr. Hart underscores the importance of cooperating with these automatic reactions, particularly the recovery system, which is often overlooked. He highlights the tendency to feel guilty when indulging in recovery, leading to neglect of this crucial aspect. Failure to cooperate with the recovery system can result in stress-related diseases, eventually taking a toll on our well-being.

The phenomenon of feeling exhausted due to prolonged stress is often referred to as "hypoadrenia," commonly known as adrenal fatigue. When we experience stress, the body releases adrenaline to help us cope with immediate threats or pressure. However, prolonged stress depletes our adrenaline reserves, leading to fatigue or tiredness. Research suggests that our bodies can sustain adrenaline-driven energy for approximately two weeks before experiencing this reversal effect.

The problem with most Americans is that we don't take enough time to recover. We live in a constant state of overstress. We keep pushing and pushing. The reason we grow tired is because that's the body's natural reaction. Our bodies are forcing us to remove ourselves from the stressors. It's when we stay in those stressful situations that we experience physical fatigue.

Another physical manifestation of burnout is *sleep disruption*. During burnout, individuals often encounter difficulties falling asleep or staying asleep. This was a personal challenge I faced during my own experience with burnout. Previously, I had never struggled with sleep, but burnout dramatically changed this. Some nights, it would take me hours to fall asleep, while others, I would wake up at 2:00 or 3:00 am and struggle to return to sleep. In some instances, I would not sleep at all throughout the night.

The severity of my sleep issues during burnout led me to seek help from my doctor. Desperate for relief, I explained my struggles with sleep and burnout and requested a sleep medication. However, my doctor cautioned against it due to potential side effects and instead prescribed Trazodone, an anti-anxiety medication. Initially skeptical, I expressed my concern that anxiety wasn't my primary issue, but he assured me of its efficacy for insomnia. While Trazodone did provide some relief, it didn't fully resolve my sleep problems. Even after recovering from burnout, I continued to grapple with sleep disturbances. The two years of battling insomnia disrupted my circadian rhythm, and though I've made progress, I'm still in the process of fully recovering from the toll it took during my burnout period.

Burnout manifests in various physical ailments, including headaches, appetite changes, stomach issues, weakened immune system, heart palpitations, hair and skin problems, muscle pains, and nausea. Despite being typically healthy and active, I found myself succumbing to more frequent colds during my burnout period. The intense physical stress I experienced took a toll on my body, compromising my immune system's ability to fend off illnesses. Even with my diligent self-care routine, the effects of burnout impacted my overall health and well-being.

Emotional Symptoms

Physical exhaustion in and of itself does not qualify as burnout. The central symptom of burnout is *emotional* exhaustion. It is an emotional fatigue that undermines people's ability to work effectively and feel positive about what they are doing. You feel drained and depleted.

This can stem from the demand of always being on, organizational culture, time pressures, or having way too much to do—especially when you lack control over your work, dislike it, or don't have the necessary skills to accomplish it. This emotional exhaustion causes an inability to concentrate or see the big picture. Even routine tasks that were once enjoyable may seem arduous, and it becomes difficult to drag yourself to work. The classic symptom of burnout happens when your emotional fuel tank runs low or dry and is not being adequately replenished.

Another common emotional symptom is *depersonalization*, also known as cynicism. My friend, Dr. Sean Gateley, experienced this symptom firsthand. He described how he became increasingly cynical and negative about his work, leading to a decline in engagement. Depersonalization serves as a psychological defense mechanism, allowing individuals to cope with their challenging circumstances.

Rather than feeling invested in their tasks, projects, colleagues, and clients, individuals experiencing depersonalization often feel detached, pessimistic, and indifferent. This persistent cynicism indicates a loss of connection, enjoyment, and pride in one's work.

Inefficacy is another emotional sign of burnout and refers to feelings of incompetence and a lack of achievement and productivity. Generally speaking, people who exhibit this symptom of burnout feel their skills slipping and worry that they won't be able to succeed or accomplish certain tasks. The sad part is you lose confidence in yourself and professional abilities. At this stage, you doubt yourself and feel like a failure. Deeper than that, you no longer find satisfaction in your work.

One of the deepest levels of emotional exhaustion is becoming *emotionally overwhelmed*. It feels hopeless and as a result, you may find yourself expressing impatience and anger. At times, you may even find yourself crying for no reason. I found myself in this pit. I can vividly recall numerous instances when I found myself alone, whether in my office, at home, in my car, or elsewhere, suddenly overcome with tears without any discernible reason. I often found myself asking, "What's wrong with me?" "Am I losing my mind?" "Could this be a nervous breakdown?"

Lack of motivation is another symptom. Not only do you no longer enjoy or engage in your work, but you find yourself losing motivation for other things that you once enjoyed doing. If you know me, you know my love for running and marathon training. However, in 2018, I noticed a significant shift in my passion. What was once a source of joy had become a burden, lacking motivation. I continued lacing up my shoes out of personal discipline rather than genuine passion. This loss of enthusiasm extended beyond running, affecting my overall zest for life. Nothing seemed to bring me joy or satisfaction anymore.

Feeling *helpless* is another significant symptom of burnout. It goes beyond a lack of passion or joy, encompassing a sense of being unable to help oneself or others. During the depths of my burnout, I felt trapped, unable to find a way out of the darkness. I questioned whether these feelings would ever dissipate. What compounded this sense of helplessness was my role in a helping profession. People, particularly in my church, relied on me to be their source of strength, guidance, and support. Yet, I found myself lacking the energy and motivation to fulfill these expectations. Instead, I grappled with guilt and self-doubt, feeling like a hypocrite for being unable to help others when I myself was struggling.

Behavioral Symptoms

A primary behavioral symptom of burnout is *reduced performance*. You no longer take pride in your work; you simply go through the motions. You may even find yourself missing meetings, taking more sick days, missing deadlines, making more mistakes, unable to focus or make decisions.

As I mentioned earlier, I was raised to have a good work ethic. I was taught to pull myself up by the bootstraps and get the dang job done. During my burnout, I was still able to fulfill my duties, but I did so without any sense of passion or investment. It became merely a job, a means to earn a paycheck and support my family. Despite outward appearances, I knew deep down that I was not fully engaged or committed to the work. Even though I showed up and went through the motions, I was aware of my diminished enthusiasm and effort. Interestingly, many leaders and individuals in my church were unaware of my internal struggles, as I managed to maintain a façade of normalcy. However, I knew the truth—that I was not giving my best, and my lack of genuine care for the work weighed heavily on me.

For those of you who are leaders, managers and supervisors in your organization, if you notice decreased productivity, absenteeism, and turnover, you are probably looking at people who are going through burnout. On the personal level, if you have noticed this pattern in yourself, accompanied with some of the other signs, you are probably in burnout. Pay attention and take action immediately.

Disconnecting and isolating from people is a behavioral sign. During my burnout experience, I hated Sunday mornings because I did not want to go to church, but I knew I had to because I was on staff. I did everything possible to avoid people. This was very significant because I am an extreme extrovert. I love people and get energized by social interactions. During this time, I just didn't have the energy to socialize and what really drained me was when I had to help people with their problems. I can remember many times when a staff member would come into my office, and ask, "Do you have a minute? I have a situation that I need your help with?" As the Business Administrator, I was the problem solver, and I can remember rolling my eyes to the ceiling when I heard that question.

About a year before I acknowledged my burnout and took a sabbatical, I developed a routine of going home alone for lunch every day. My home became my sanctuary, a place where I sought solace and regained some semblance of peace amidst the chaos of my professional life. This retreat allowed me to recharge and prepare myself mentally for the remainder of the workday. However, this behavior also marked a significant withdrawal from social interaction—a classic symptom of burnout. For me, this withdrawal was not solely physical; it was accompanied by a deep emotional retreat. Fueled by pride and a fear of judgment, I hesitated to confide in others about my struggles. I felt isolated and misunderstood, lacking the trust and support necessary to open up about my experiences.

Burnout can also place significant strain on relationships with colleagues, friends, and family members, often leading to increased irritability and withdrawal. Throughout my experience with burnout, I found myself becoming increasingly impatient and quick-tempered. Minor annoyances that I once handled with grace and professionalism now seemed to provoke an outsized reaction from me. I became acutely aware of the negative changes in my demeanor and disliked the person I was becoming. To avoid potential outbursts of anger and conflict, I began to withdraw from interpersonal interactions altogether.

Unfortunately, the behavioral symptoms of burnout can have devastating consequences, potentially leading individuals to turn to alcohol and other substances as a coping mechanism. Dr. Sean Gateley candidly admitted to alcohol abuse during his own journey through burnout, recalling periods of binge drinking on his days off. This pattern of behavior is not uncommon among those grappling with the intense pressures of burnout. Personally, I managed to avoid this pitfall—though in hindsight, perhaps a drink or two wouldn't have hurt!

In my research for this book, I encountered numerous accounts of individuals whose experiences with burnout ended tragically. Some saw their marriages dissolve, while others succumbed to addiction or financial ruin. Burnout has a way of distorting one's judgment, making it crucial to recognize its symptoms and understand its various stages. Herbert Freudenberger, an American psychologist, first introduced the concept of burnout syndrome in the 1970s, laying the groundwork for Dr. Paula Redmond, a Clinical Psychologist, to develop the 5 Stages of Burnout. Identifying which stage one is in can facilitate the appropriate interventions to prevent reaching a breaking point.

Let's briefly examine these stages:

The Honeymoon Phase: This is the phase of energy, optimism, and productivity. Typically, when we enter a new job, we do so with high job satisfaction, commitment, energy, and creativity. At first, this could be healthy, but if you over-function and do not pace yourself, you can drive yourself into burnout. As a marathoner, you do not want to go out too fast the first half of the marathon. The beginning of a marathon can be very exciting. You are pumped, full of energy, and, when you start running, you are motivated by the spectators and other runners. Since you are well-trained, it feels easy at first. Many runners, and myself included, have been deceived by the energy of the first few miles. If you are not too careful, you can get caught up in a pace that you cannot sustain, so you hit the wall the last few miles of the race. Initially, burnout can be quite subtle. You might enter a new job with high levels of enthusiasm, overworking and over-functioning, believing you can sustain this pace for years. However, without careful attention, you may unknowingly be laying the groundwork for burnout down the line.

The Onset of Stress Phase: This is the beginning of emotional and physical stress. As we have already established, stress is not necessarily burnout, but prolonged stress will lead to burnout. In this stage, you will discover that your optimism, energy and satisfaction begin to wane. You don't live in stress every day and it doesn't have adverse effects at first, but if you are not paying attention, you will continue to move down the stages.

The Chronic Stress Phase: At this stage, you will begin to feel stress more persistently. There will be a marked change in your stress levels. It becomes more intense. The physical, mental, emotional, and behavioral symptoms begin to emerge.

The Burnout Phase: Now, you are in burnout! You have finally reached your limit. The energy, optimism, and productivity you felt in the beginning are long gone. This is the critical phase. It is important to address the symptoms in the Chronic Stress Phase, so you don't reach this point. If you missed it, now is the time to stop the slide. Take action and steps for intervention.

The Habitual Burnout Phase: At this stage, burnout becomes ingrained in your daily routine. You find yourself in a situation reminiscent of where I and Dr. Sean Gateley once stood. If left unaddressed, this is the point where you risk becoming overwhelmed and inevitably crashing into the proverbial wall.

Just as responsible drivers heed the warning lights on their vehicles—such as the "check engine," "low tire," or "oil" indicators—attentiveness to burnout signs is crucial. These signals serve as alarms, alerting us to potential issues that require our attention and care. My aim is to equip you with the knowledge to recognize these signs and stages clearly, empowering you to steer clear of the flames of burnout.

CHAPTER 5

HOW TO PREVENT BURNOUT

We live life going forward, but we learn from life looking backward. The signs of burnout are now glaringly obvious to me in hindsight. Moreover, I can trace the progression of my condition, observing how it worsened over time. In fact, even before reaching the point typically defined as burnout, I can recognize the early indicators pointing me in that direction.

I believe if I had been more self-aware, I would have paid attention to the smoke and flares; instead, I had to live through the blaze and flames. It's unfortunate because I truly believe that if I had been self-aware and committed to addressing my mental and emotional health, I could have prevented burnout entirely.

I want you to learn from my experience and be aware of the early warning signs. I do believe that if you recognize the early warning signs and do something about it, you can avoid what I and thousands of others have been through. This chapter will not delve into technicalities. Instead, it will offer highly practical advice.

Burnout is bigger than just working long hours, although that can contribute to burnout. There are organizational, work-related and environmental factors that cause burnout. Burnout happens because of a certain mindset and lifestyle. The good news is you don't have to go through burnout. You can prevent it by managing your life properly.

Focus on Self-Care

Self-care is your responsibility. It is my hope that your company values employees enough to encourage self-care and that they offer wellness resources. But at the end of the day, taking care of yourself is on you. No one else can love you better than you. No one else can care for you better than you.

I have known, talked to, and interviewed many people who have gone through burnout and, in every narrative, there is one constant theme: they did not focus on self-care. I want to expose and challenge the myth that practicing self-care is selfish. Nothing could be further from the truth. Self-care is often perceived as being selfish, especially among those of us in helping professions.

We shoulder the responsibility of caring for others, which is noble and necessary. It's true that we're here to assist, support, invest in, and nurture others, leaving a lasting impact. However, I want to challenge the notion that we should do so at the expense of neglecting ourselves. While caring for others, we must also prioritize our own well-being. The reality is that if we are healthy ourselves, we'll be better equipped to care for others effectively.

Burnout is a "drained" condition. We become drained when we constantly give without replenishing ourselves. We find ourselves serving and working on an empty tank, unknowingly damaging our internal engine. Eventually, we reach a point where we have nothing left to give because the resources we draw from—physical, psychological, emotional, social, and spiritual—have dried up. Prolonged periods of serving and working with empty tanks in these areas lead us into burnout.

One way we can focus on self-care is to exercise. That may sound a bit strange to some of you because when you exercise, you are actually *exerting* energy. But exercise can actually *replenish* your physical and emotional energy. When you are physically healthy, you feel better and you're better able to focus and tap into positive energy for your work. Exercise releases hormones and endorphins that energize you.

Personally, I love running. I find a lot of joy training for marathons and I get energized by the very thought of running. Some of you are probably thinking, "this guy is nuts." I agree – I am. People who think that of me usually are those who hate running. I get that. Running is not for everyone. There are many options when it comes to forms of exercising. Here's the key: find an activity that you enjoy. If you enjoy it, you will stick with it and it can become a life-long pattern.

Find an activity that is fun for you. That could be walking, swimming, playing pick-up basketball with friends, hiking, racquetball, weightlifting... the list goes on. There's a lot of excitement surrounding a relatively new sport called pickleball. While I haven't played it myself, I've heard it's incredibly enjoyable. Thousands of Americans are flocking to pickleball courts to take part in this trend. However, the specific activity you choose isn't as important as ensuring it's something you genuinely enjoy and eagerly anticipate. The crucial factor is consistency—aim to engage in your chosen activity regularly, ideally at least three times a week.

Not only will exercising keep you fit and healthy, but it's also a good distraction. If you are working in a job that's particularly stressful and one that you're not enjoying, exercising takes your mind off of it. When you are finished exercising, you will feel better about yourself and where you are in life. It will also give you a much better mindset because of those "feel good" hormones and endorphins that are produced from exercising.

During my burnout, I was under stress and I didn't like my job, but running was one of the things that kept me sane. As I discussed earlier in this book, I persevered through my work despite experiencing burnout. One of the coping mechanisms I relied on was looking forward to my post-work runs. The revitalizing energy I derived from running provided me with just enough fuel to navigate through another day. I highly recommend making exercise a cornerstone of your routine. Treat it with the same level of importance as any other commitment by scheduling it into your calendar every week.

It's crucial to prioritize nutrition, as many nutritionists emphasize the connection between our moods and our gut health. Personally, I've been committed to healthy eating for most of my adult life. I admit one of the reasons is vanity; maintaining my ideal weight is important to me. Please refrain from judging me or hating me, but at the age of 60, I still weigh the same as I did in high school.

Portion control is paramount. Even with the right food choices, overeating can still occur. Focus on incorporating plenty of vegetables, fruits, lean proteins, and complex carbohydrates into your diet.

Limiting alcohol and caffeine intake while staying hydrated with plenty of water is also essential.

Another crucial component of preventing burnout is ensuring you get plenty of sleep. This is vital because once burnout sets in, sleep issues and insomnia can become significant problems, as I experienced firsthand. Consistently inadequate sleep can elevate your risk for long-term and chronic health issues.

During sleep, your body works to support healthy brain function and maintain physical health. It enhances cognitive function, sharpens reflexes, and boosts focus. Additionally, adequate sleep plays a pivotal role in reducing stress and improving mood.

Sleep isn't just important for mitigating the risk of serious health conditions like diabetes and heart disease; it also helps alleviate stress and enhance mood. This is because during sleep, nerve cells in the brainstem release neurotransmitters such as norepinephrine, histamine, and serotonin. Serotonin, in particular, is a natural chemical that regulates mood, emotions, and overall sense of well-being.

To prevent burnout, experts recommend adults aim for between 7 and 9 hours of sleep per night. Those who consistently sleep less than 7 hours may face more health issues than those who get sufficient rest. Adequate sleep plays a crucial role in burnout prevention by promoting the production of serotonin, which reduces anxiety and enhances mood. Therefore, if your job or life is stressful, prioritizing adequate sleep can help you cope with stressors and reduce the risk of burnout.

Taking regular breaks is another effective strategy for preventing burnout. It's essential to avoid working at home after hours, on weekends, or during vacations. Utilize all the vacation time provided by your company, even if they compensate for unused days. The benefits of time off outweigh the financial compensation. Many employees leave vacation time unused, but this practice is detrimental to mental health. Taking breaks allows for much-needed refreshment and renewal, essential for preventing burnout.

When I became the Business Administrator at the church where I was serving, I left a job that provided me with 4 weeks of vacation. The church gave me 2 weeks, even though I had 30 years of experience and was in a senior leadership position. I asked the board for 2 additional weeks when we were negotiating salary and benefits, but they denied it. A couple of years into the job, after getting settled in and learning the demands of the job, I went to my supervisor and asked if he would go back to the board to advocate for me to receive an additional 2 weeks of vacation. He refused. I thought after proving myself and working hard, the senior leader and board would be open to it.

How wrong I was. Their decision dampened my spirit. I didn't feel cared for. I wondered how I would survive the demands with only 2 weeks of vacation a year. The expectations were high, the demands were great, and the responsibilities were overwhelming. I believe that one of the reasons that I went through burnout was simply not having enough time to refresh. The time off that I had was not enough to rejuvenate. I did take all of my time off, but it still wasn't enough for the demands and expectations that I had.

I've found that people who do not focus on self-care generally do not have hobbies. It is important to exercise, eat right, sleep properly, and take your time off—but it is also important to have at least one hobby. Having a hobby brings balance to your life and helps you to mentally shut down when you are not at work. Find a fun hobby. There are so many options for hobbies. Your hobby needs to be something other than exercising, despite how much you may enjoy your exercise activity. Your hobby needs to be something that you are good at and skilled at. That gives you meaning and helps you to feel good about yourself.

When we experience a less than ideal working situation, we tend to feel demoralized. Having a hobby that we are skilled at and passionate about helps mitigate some of the feelings of demoralization. Hobbies also provide space for healthy distractions and detachment from your work. They help you realize that you are more than just your work. Self-care is essential in establishing work-life balance.

Achieving work-life balance is an ongoing process that is rarely perfect. There will be periods when work demands more of your time, and other times when you feel a sense of equilibrium. The key isn't to strive for perfection but to establish boundaries that prevent you from becoming consumed by work and neglecting other aspects of your life. Work-life balance involves recognizing when to dedicate yourself to work and when to prioritize leisure and personal time. It's about finding a rhythm that works for you, even if it's not flawless, to prevent becoming overly fixated on work.

Shift Your Perspective

While rest, relaxation, and replenishment are essential for mitigating exhaustion, reducing cynicism, and enhancing efficacy, they may not fully resolve the underlying causes of burnout. In the workplace, you may continue to encounter demanding workloads, toxic cultures, contentious team dynamics, and unrealistic expectations, which can perpetuate burnout despite efforts to prioritize self-care.

You have to find ways to manage the things that you cannot control. Your workload may not change and the culture of your company may be a long way from becoming healthy. In this situation, it then comes down to your mindset.

Under the right circumstances, and by that I mean, you have an empathetic boss and you work in a healthy culture, I recommend going to your boss and expressing what you are feeling. Ask for help. Open the discussion about shifting some responsibilities. Find out what your boss can do to help you lighten the load and remove some of the factors that may lead to burnout later.

One idea I considered but never pursued was proposing changes to my job description to my boss. I had a plan outlined, even written down, but I hesitated to bring it up because I didn't feel psychologically safe. My lack of trust stemmed from comments my boss made about burnout, expressing disbelief in its existence. With this skepticism in mind, I chose to keep my feelings and potential solutions to myself.

After reflecting on my situation, I began to ask myself how I could infuse more joy and fulfillment into my job. *How could I reignite my passion for my work?* I started delegating tasks where possible, allowing me to focus more on the aspects of my job that brought me fulfillment. While some tasks were unavoidable, I found ways to streamline them for efficiency, freeing up more time for activities I enjoyed. I took control of what I could control.

One significant contributor to my burnout was managing challenging personalities that often led to conflict and drama. To shift my perspective, I decided to minimize my interactions with these individuals and instead focus more on collaborating with positive team members. The draining negativity from the difficult personalities took a toll on me, so I chose to engage with them only when necessary.

There are situations when you need to start looking for another job. Clearly, people do leave jobs because they are emotionally exhausted and depleted. However, that's not always an option. In these cases, you have to reduce exposure to job stressors by minimizing time spent with difficult personalities and time spent in the areas that you are not as passionate about.

Build Nurturing Social Connections

Isolation can manifest in various forms during burnout, including both physical and emotional withdrawal. Physical isolation involves consciously distancing oneself from others, while emotional isolation entails feeling lonely despite being in regular contact with people. Both types of isolation are common experiences during burnout and can exacerbate feelings of disconnection and loneliness.

To prevent burnout, it is important to have a wide range of friends. I believe that meaningful friendships can be established in the workplace. The sense of well-being, inclusion, and feeling connected is important for enjoying your work. The sense of being a part of a team, collaboration, mutual care, respect and belonging are the things that make working in a place meaningful. You need to enjoy the work that you do, but you also need to enjoy the people with whom you are working.

To build nurturing relationships at work can be summed up in two words: intentionality and initiative. Relationships just don't happen or develop. It requires intentional work. It also means you have to take the initiative in nurturing those friendships. I recommend participating in social activities outside of work. You don't need to do this with *everyone* on your team. There are some people that we just naturally feel drawn to because of emotional connection, synergy, and chemistry. Find those people and invite them to socialize with you outside of work. Go out to dinner, invite them to your home, go to events, and find other fun opportunities to be with them outside of work. Some of the best friendships I have had have been forged in the workplace. Don't isolate yourself.

It's crucial to cultivate deep and meaningful friendships outside of the workplace. These friendships provide a safe space to share frustrations and concerns without fear of workplace repercussions. Having friends outside of work offers a fresh perspective and ensures psychological safety, as conversations remain confidential and free from office politics.

However, the significance of these friendships extends beyond venting frustrations. They also contribute to enjoyment, mutual support, and emotional connection, enriching life outside of work. Building a diverse network of friends, ranging from casual acquaintances to close confidants, is essential for emotional well-being. Human beings thrive on relationships, and nurturing these connections adds meaning and fulfillment to life. Research shows that individuals with strong social networks are less prone to burnout compared to those who are socially isolated.

Set Realistic Boundaries

My neighbor and I recently upgraded our shared fence by having a vinyl fence installed. The old iron fence, dating back to 1989 when our neighborhood was constructed, had started to deteriorate, prompting the decision for a replacement. Besides the fence's deteriorating condition, privacy was also a concern. The open design of the iron fence allowed full visibility into each other's yards, which we both found intrusive.

The installation of the new vinyl fence, standing at a solid 6 feet high, has resolved the privacy issue entirely. We are both pleased with the outcome and enjoy the newfound privacy it provides to our respective backyards.

The fence serves another crucial purpose: it delineates the boundaries between my property and my neighbor's. Just as he is responsible for what falls within his side of the fence, I'm accountable for maintaining my side. This physical barrier clearly demarcates ownership and responsibility, mirroring the function of relational boundaries.

Boundary issues are common and can manifest in two ways: disregarding others' boundaries or failing to establish our own. The challenge lies in navigating potentially uncomfortable conversations and overcoming feelings of guilt or fear that accompany boundary-setting. However, proper boundary-setting is essential for maintaining healthy relationships and safeguarding our well-being.

It's common to struggle with setting boundaries with friends, parents, children, in-laws, and other important people in our lives. Perhaps one of the most difficult places to set boundaries is in the workplace. The fear of damaging relationships with colleagues or superiors often prevents us from setting boundaries in the workplace. We may also feel guilty, especially considering the compensation and benefits we receive. However, it's crucial to recognize that our employer doesn't own us. Our responsibility is to fulfill our job description competently, not to sacrifice our well-being. While exceptional employees may go above and beyond, it's essential to establish boundaries to protect ourselves. Without proper boundaries, we open ourselves up to the risk of burnout.

What does this look like in the workplace? Some employees pick up the slack for employees who do not do their job in an effort to protect them or to protect the team. But that's not your responsibility—especially if it's at the expense of your well-being. There are times when a colleague needs your help. As a loyal and committed team member, there is nothing wrong with helping them. But when they push the *full load* on you, that is NOT your responsibility. It is theirs.

It's also imperative to set boundaries around how much work you do at home after hours, on weekends, and on vacation. I drive my family crazy when we go on vacation because I never have my phone on me. My family members are on their cell phones texting friends, surfing the internet, interacting on social media, and taking photos of all the beautiful sites we get to see on vacation. I leave my phone in my hotel room because, when I am on vacation, I completely unplug. I don't respond to anyone unless it is urgent or an emergency. I make it a point to check my phone in the evenings only for urgent matters. Anything else can wait until I return home.

My family often questions why I do this, and you might be wondering the same thing. The reason is simple: it's about reclaiming my time. I need those vacations to refresh, renew, and replenish my soul and spirit. This downtime is essential for me to return to work rejuvenated, fresh, and fully engaged. If I remained plugged into work during my vacation, the purpose of taking time off would be diminished.

I take this boundary seriously. My previous boss didn't understand it, and there was a cost, but it was a price I was willing to pay. Once, I was reprimanded by him because I didn't respond while I was on vacation. My response to him was simple: "I never contact you when you are on vacation, so I expect the same from you."

While boundaries may not be difficult to set, they can be challenging to maintain. We don't have any problems setting boundaries, but when they are challenged, we have a tendency to cave because we don't want to disappoint the other person or we feel guilty. People who are used to getting their way may get mad when we set boundaries because they feel like their power is being taken away. I believe that is what my previous boss felt. He was not empowered to control me while I was on vacation and he did not like that. It is important to remember that we are not responsible for other people's emotions. We are only responsible for our own well-being.

Establish Time Management Practices

Chaos breeds chaos! When we work in a busy environment with heavy workloads, constant interruptions, unmanageable expectations and it feels chaotic, we manage it by bringing some control and order to our schedules. We make it even more chaotic by not having the proper systems to get it all done.

Establishing solid time management practices will help you avoid burnout. Managing your time will reduce your stress level through time control. It does not reduce the amount of work that you do, but it will help you manage your work.

Time management practices will also help you bring balance between your work and personal life. The balance will come because time management begins with determining what is most important in your life. It is important to make yourself important. Many professionals only use time management principles and practices in their work. Solid time management practices allow you to set priorities around your personal life, as well as your professional life.

I want to refer to Stephen Covey's work on this. In *The 7 Habits of Highly Effective People*, he talks about the four quadrants:

> **Quadrant 1:** This quadrant represents necessity. Items in this quadrant take priority because they are essential. Covey refers to these as urgent and necessary. Constantly dealing with the tyranny of the urgent can lead to burnout because we're always reacting to crises or emergencies. Often, we're pulled away from important tasks to address these urgent matters.
>
> **Quadrant 2:** This quadrant represents quality. Here lie the tasks that are not urgent but are highly important to us. It's where we should allocate most of our time. This includes the aspects of our job that we're deeply passionate about, critical to the company, and contribute to overall quality. It's also where we should prioritize ourselves. Your personal life should be scheduled into your calendar and to-do lists. If something doesn't make it onto your calendar or list, it's likely not a priority for you. Self-care belongs in quadrant 2 because YOU ARE IMPORTANT!

Quadrant 3: This quadrant is the realm of deception. Tasks here are urgent but not important. Their urgency can deceive us into believing they are significant. However, we must handle them swiftly and efficiently before shifting our focus to more crucial matters.

Quadrant 4: This quadrant represents waste. Tasks here are neither urgent nor important. Much of our stress may stem from spending excessive time on trivial matters, diverting attention from more significant priorities. Identifying and minimizing time-wasting activities is crucial for maximizing productivity.

Time management is about determining your values and priorities. Make a list of your most important priorities—personal and professional—and get those things on your calendar and task lists first.

Before moving to the next chapter, I want you to write a brief strategy about how you are going to prevent burnout. I gave you five strategies for preventing burnout. I want you to spend some time reflecting on those five strategies and write an action step that you are going to take for each:

Self-care: I am going to________________________

Shift my perspective: I am going to________________

Build Social Connections: I am going to__________

Set realistic boundaries: I am going to___________

Time Management Practice: I am going to________

Now, if you are already in burnout, I invite you to move to the next chapter where I'm going to share how you can recover from your burnout. There is hope. I experienced the flames of burnout and recovered—you are going to as well, so let's keep reading.

CHAPTER 6

HOW TO RECOVER FROM BURNOUT

It was a Saturday morning and I had just finished a run with my running buddies. When I got in my car to return home, I checked my phone, and saw I had a message from a board member of a private high school. He called to say that Carl Martinez, the Head of Schools, was in burnout and needed support and guidance.

This was a year after my own burnout recovery. I had already started my new business of consulting, training, and coaching leaders. After getting home, I called the board member back to see how I could pitch in. He informed me that Carl was granted a 12-week leave, and they were looking to hire a coach to help him recover from burnout.

This board member was familiar with my experience and recovery. He also knew that coaching leaders was not only a passion of mine, but was now what I did professionally. He indicated that the board would like to hire me to coach Carl by coming alongside him, supporting him, and resourcing him. I agreed, submitted a proposal, and took on the responsibility.

After the board accepted my proposal and fee, I contacted Carl for an intake meeting. I didn't know Carl at the time, but we immediately hit it off. I asked questions about his journey and about his burnout.

Carl was open, honest, and vulnerable. I learned a lot about him as he offered some clues as to how he ended up in burnout. He had been at the school for 25 years and was under tremendous pressure to keep enrollment up and raise money for the school. Both of these responsibilities are important to and challenging for private schools. Carl was exhausted.

Sadly, Carl had been in burnout three years before the board decided that he needed to take some time off. That is a *long time* to keep working and straining without addressing his condition. But that's Carl's personality. He has high initiative, a strong sense of responsibility, a strong work ethic, and he drives himself. He felt he couldn't let the school down, so he continued straining and struggling.

Over the course of those three years, each day, week, and month was simply about survival. He explained that he had grown numb to his mental, physical, emotional, and spiritual state. While negative effects were evident in each area, he managed to conceal them from most people within his circle of influence and leadership. However, his family and close associates were aware of the severity of his situation and recognized that he was in distress.

Certainly, Carl's work environment played a significant role in fostering conditions conducive to burnout, such as the pressure to maintain enrollment and secure donations for the school. However, internal factors also contributed. Carl's type-A personality, characterized by high expectations of both himself and others, exacerbated the situation. We now find it amusing, but one of the initial observations I made to him was he enjoys living on adrenaline rushes. He derived satisfaction from staying busy and working under pressure. Eventually, this lifestyle became unsustainable. While not quite a micromanager, Carl had a tendency to involve himself in all aspects of the school's operations, a habit not explicitly expected by the board or staff but self-imposed due to his strong sense of responsibility. This tendency diverted his focus from higher-level leadership responsibilities.

I met with Carl during his three-month leave of absence and continued working with him a year after he returned to his role. At the beginning of our coaching partnership, I worked with him on developing a recovery plan. Carl wasn't doing a good job of managing stress; he wasn't taking care of himself physically, spending time with friends, taking time off or engaging in hobbies. In other words, his work-life balance was way out of sorts. His life was: WORK, WORK, and more WORK. I gave him resources to read and we put together a recovery plan that brought life back into balance. The purpose was to get him into recovery-mode, but also to re-balance his life and establish rhythms that would sustain him for the rest of his life and career.

In each session, we talked through how he was doing in executing his plan. I helped him process his feelings and why he was experiencing burnout. I held him accountable to his recovery and recalibration. Carl received both support and accountability from me. Accountability was important because, with his personality, it would've been very easy for him to revert back to his natural tendencies and rhythm.

He was the "perfect" coaching client. He showed up prepared for each meeting, made progress and was always ready to engage in some hard conversations about where he was. After a month of meeting with him, he looked different. He looked happy. He looked peaceful. It was like night and day. The first time I met with Carl, he looked awful and beaten up. Within just a month, it was evident that Carl was making remarkable strides simply from his appearance. He was in the process of recalibrating his life, mindset, habits, and rhythms.

Carl's journey is a testament to success. Upon returning to work, he was fully recovered, rekindling his sense of purpose and passion. Not only did he overcome burnout, but he also revamped his work approach. Implementing new practices, he reorganized internal staff roles and redistributed responsibilities. Today, he operates as the Head of School at a more strategic level, trusting his capable staff and recognizing that he doesn't need to micromanage every detail.

Carl's work-life balance is now a priority for him. He focuses on self-care by exercising, engaging in hobbies, and spending quality time with family. He also takes time off when he needs to. Carl is in a better place now and is poised to live a quality life and have a fulfilling career in education. If you are struggling with burnout, I hope you find Carl's story to be encouraging. His story is one of hope and resilience.

Recovering from burnout is a complex and highly individualized process influenced by various factors, including the severity of burnout, individual resilience, workplace support, and self-care practices.

Recovering from burnout takes time, patience, and effort. It is important to be gentle with yourself and trust that with the right strategies and support, you can overcome burnout and cultivate a greater sense of well-being, just like my friend Carl.

Often, I'm asked how long it takes to recover from burnout. It varies depending on the individual and the severity of burnout. Mild cases may resolve relatively quickly with the proper self-care and support. Severe burnout may require an extended recovery period and even professional intervention.

The duration of recovery from burnout varies depending on several factors, including workplace support and individual self-care practices. Supportive workplaces that offer resources and services can expedite recovery by providing tools to address burnout-related issues. However, personal resilience and engagement in self-care practices also play significant roles in the recovery process.

Individuals who prioritize self-care can replenish their physical and emotional resources more effectively, potentially shortening their recovery time. Additionally, personal resilience levels influence how quickly someone can bounce back from burnout. Due to the diverse ways in which burnout impacts individuals, recovery times can range from a few weeks to several years.

A 2021 clinical perspective paper that noted previous research has found that many individuals with mild burnout recover within 3 months. A 2016 study by Maslach and Leiter found the average recovery time from burnout ranged from several weeks to several months, depending on the severity of burnout and individual factors.

Research by Bianchi et al. (2018) suggested that individuals who actively engaged in self-care practices and received social support experienced faster recovery from burnout compared to those who did not.

Additional research suggests that not only is recovery time determined by a person's level of resilience, social support, professional support and self-care, but the specific field or industry can play a role. A 2018 study by Schaufeli and Enzmann indicated that burnout recovery time varied among different occupational groups, with some professions requiring longer recovery periods than others.

Throughout this book, I've mentioned taking a 10-week leave of absence from my job. During that period, I made a concerted effort towards my recovery. I prioritized activities that rejuvenated me, such as sleeping in, going for runs, engaging in hobbies like home projects, spending time with friends, journaling, and participating in a support group to process my experiences, which I'll delve into later. Additionally, I sought support from professionals.

Those 10 weeks were essential and certainly beneficial. By the end of it, I no longer felt drained and depleted, although there were still some lingering issues that required further attention. Reflecting on my leave of absence now, I see it as a crucial step in halting the decline and initiating long-term healing. It was like putting a bandage on an open wound, allowing it to scab over. However, as with any wound, simply covering it is not enough. Continued intentionality and effort are necessary for ongoing recovery and healing.

For me, total and complete healing didn't come until almost a year later. One of my most profound physical symptoms was insomnia. My sleep cycle was so bad. It got better during my leave of absence, but I still struggled with sleep months after. If I can be honest with you, it has been over four years, and my sleep is still not where it was before my burnout.

Certainly, after hearing Carl's story and discussing the varying recovery timelines, it's time to delve into practical strategies for recovery. I'll share six principles, which I've gleaned from my personal experience and shared with clients to aid in overcoming burnout. Let's refer to these principles as the "6 R's."

1. The Principle of Rest

On a car, you have to fix the flat tire before you can move on. Burnout is like having a flat tire. I believe one of the most important elements of recovery is rest. I also believe that regardless of the severity of burnout, it is important to take some time off. In mild cases, that may mean an extended vacation. In severe cases, it is a longer leave of absence.

Burnout is a combination of physical and emotional exhaustion, but primarily an emotional condition of exhaustion. It is a state of feeling drained, depleted and demoralized. The only way to restore the body, mind and spirit is to take a break.

There are two important issues that I need to share in this section. The first is you need to acknowledge and accept where you are. Recognize that you are experiencing burnout and accept it without judging and criticizing yourself. Understand that it is a common experience and does not reflect failure on your part. You need to give yourself permission to take a break.

My friend, Carl, had a hard time with this. He could not give himself permission to acknowledge and accept where he was physically and emotionally, and as a result, ended up working in a drained state and condition for 3 years. I had the exact mentality. I waited 2 years before accepting that I was in burnout and before I decided to take some time off.

The other issue is getting the support and resources needed from your employer. As a Business Consultant, I want to address leaders of organizations. Focus on burnout prevention for your employees. Set up resources, training, wellness programs and support systems to help your employees prevent burnout.

As an employee, be courageous and go to your supervisor if you are experiencing burnout. Don't be afraid of asking for help and time off. It took me two years to develop enough courage to do this. In my previous career, burnout was a sign of weakness or a sickness, which kept me from asking for help and addressing my burnout earlier. I had to get to a breaking point. When I finally did it, continuing to work as a fried, burned out employee was not an option. I had to do it to get healthy.

A number of burned out employees are reluctant to ask for time off to address burnout because of consequences. In most states, employees are *eligible* to take a stress leave. If you are struggling with workplace related stress, depression, anxiety, or burnout, you qualify for a leave of absence.

Under FMLA, you can take up to 12 work weeks for stress. This is designed to give employees time away from work to take care of their physical and mental health. This is different from vacation time. Stress leave is for when a few days off aren't enough to reduce your stress levels and refuel your emotional tank.

A stress leave from work is a personal decision. It is important to prioritize your mental and emotional health and wellbeing. If you are feeling burnout, don't hesitate to take advantage of this resource that is at your disposal. Go to your Human Resources Department and let them know that you would like to take an FMLA approved absence for stress leave. They will provide you with the necessary paperwork that you must take to your doctor.

As noted in one of my earlier chapters, our society has done a major disservice in the treatment and recovery of burnout because of stigmatizing. It requires courage and vulnerability to admit burnout. When you go to your supervisor, it is up to you how much you want to disclose; however, it is not different from reporting a physical health problem. In communicating to your supervisor, share what you are feeling and be specific about what is being affected.

In that conversation, you may have to educate your boss on what burnout is and what it is not. Refer to chapter 1 and explain that burnout is not a mental illness or a nervous breakdown. Help your boss understand that it is a condition or state of emotional exhaustion that requires intentional intervention to overcome, which may mean time off. Rest is crucial in stopping the slide and paving the road for recovery.

2. The Principle of Reflection

At the end of week 1 of my sabbatical or leave of absence, I remember thinking how much I was going to enjoy time off. For 30 years, I was in a constant grind, except for 2 or 3 weeks throughout the year on family vacations. Over the years, we have had some amazing vacations, but our vacations were never restful. They were super fun, but not restful. My wife and I enjoy touring sites and seeing things. We are not the types to lie around the pool or on the beach. We are always doing things.

This was different. I also remember feeling relief because I didn't have to worry about managing staff, going to meetings, planning activities, overseeing the budget and all of the other things that were associated with my job. During my leave, one of the things that I did every single day was sit for about 2 hours to pray, think, reflect and process life. I also went out and bought a notebook and labeled it *"My Burnout Journal"*. Every day, as I reflected on where I was in my life, I recorded my thoughts and feelings. I still have that notebook, and I refer to it often. It's a reminder of a very significant and turning point of my life. I have many memories of my burnout experience and recovery period, but I am glad that I captured them on paper.

If you are recovering from burnout. I encourage you to do the same. Spend time each day reflecting on where you are, what you are thinking and what you are feeling. Write down your thoughts and feelings. This helps your perspective and is an important step toward your healing and recovery.

I did some hard and honest reflection on why I burned out. I am going to be frank with you and tell you that this is painful, because you have to look deep in your heart and soul. Anytime we do deep personal reflection, it creates discomfort because we honestly and critically look at ourselves. This is not only important for healing the emotional damage caused by burnout, but it also sets the foundation for making corrections. I didn't like it, but for the first time in my life, I actually saw the cracks in my armor, which led me into the flames of burnout. Perfectionism, people pleasing, lack of boundaries, neglecting self and other things came to light.

We learn by looking backward, but we live by looking forward. My reflections went beyond looking backward. I also looked ahead and thought about what I really wanted for my life. What is my true purpose in life? What are my passions and what do I enjoy? What do I want to spend the rest of my life doing? What is the best way to make a contribution and leave a legacy?

Reflecting gives the brain an opportunity to pause amidst the chaos, and sort through our experiences. Unfortunately, in the hustle and bustle of life, we do not take the time to do that. It was Socrates who once said, "The unexamined life is not worth living."

3. The Principle of Recalibration

Think about the things that need calibration. There are clamp meters, insulation testers, thermometers, calipers, data acquisition systems, gas detectors, torque wrenches, barometers, and other items and equipment. The primary function of calibration is to maintain accuracy, standardization and repeatability in measurements. The things that require calibration have to be re-calibrated at times. Without regular calibration, equipment can fall out of spec, provide inaccurate measurements and threaten quality.

Burnout is a huge threat to the quality of our lives. To recalibrate means that we correct, fix or amend the things that are wrong in our lives. To recalibrate yourself means that you change the way you do things or think about something.

As a part of my reflection during my leave of absence, a big question was "what do I need to re-calibrate?" Obviously, there were some things that were wrong that needed to be fixed, otherwise, I would not have gone into burnout. Let me pause here and give you a warning. If you are in burnout and have decided to take a leave of absence, rest alone is not the answer. You can sleep in everyday, play, have fun, watch your favorite television shows, hang out with friends and enjoy a plethora of other activities. But if you do not think about what needs to be changed, you will go back to work physically rested and emotionally replenished, but in a few months, you may find yourself back in burnout. Why? Because you did not change anything. You went back to work under the same circumstances, with the same mindset and same rhythms.

What should you consider in the re-calibration process? You have to go back to both the external and internal factors that led you into burnout. The internal piece was easy for me because I felt that I had complete control in making the needed changes. Where I struggled was with the external factors or my work environment. I realized that I couldn't change the personalities of difficult staff members. I understood that I couldn't eliminate programs. I was fully aware that I could not change the leadership style of my boss, who was a micromanager. So, what could I do to manage these things?

On the internal side, I journaled some strategies that addressed my type-A personality, perfectionism, people pleasing mindset and need to prove myself. Although I knew that I would have to unlearn some things, break old habits and ways of thinking, I knew I could manage what was wrong inside of me.

What I am about to write is one of the reasons I believe I was terminated after my sabbatical. I thought of ways that I could manage the external factor that caused my burnout. That one thing was managing the difficult personalities on staff. If it had been up to me, I would have just fired them, but I did not have the authority to do so. My strategy was to be more confrontational with these specific staff members, address their behavior and put consequences in place. I truly believe that would have mitigated a lot of the staff drama.

Unfortunately, that did not go over well when I communicated it. To back up for a moment, the board created an evaluation team of three people, the senior leader, and two board members. They were charged with the responsibility of evaluating my recovery and fitness to return to my position, which I thought was a bit odd. One of the questions that they asked was how I planned to manage the drama, conflict and unhealthy culture of the staff. I shared my plan and approach. They didn't like it. I was hit with, "we are a church and that is not the way we handle things around here!" You see, I believe that when it comes to culture, you get what you put up with. The Senior Leader not only loved drama, but refused to address the negative attitudes about staff. At that moment, I knew I was between a rock and a hard place. I realized that if I returned to my job, nothing was going to change with the situation I had to manage. This is a good place to segue to the next principle.

4. The Principle of Re-evaluation

When you experience job burnout, you have to evaluate if you are in the right position and right environment. After the meeting with the evaluation team, I began weighing my options. I wondered if I should even go back to my position after my sabbatical. If I had to manage the same drama that led to my burnout, I would probably be back into burnout in a few months.

Throughout my sabbatical, I did think about not returning to my job so I could start my own consulting business and be a self-employed entrepreneur. The thought of doing that frightened me, but it especially threatened my wife's sense of security. Throughout my recovery process, it was a dream and even an option, but in my mind, it was far-fetched from becoming a reality. Do I have what it takes to start my own business? Could I make money doing it? After the meeting with the evaluation team, I thought seriously about it because I had a feeling that they might decide to terminate me.

If I can be transparent, if they had asked me to come back, I probably would have returned to my job, because of my own fear and my wife's reservations about me starting a business. Could I really just walk away from a job with a 6-figure salary and great benefits? Would my wife hate me for doing that?

My point is if you experienced job related stress that drove you into burnout, you have to consider changing jobs, especially if it is not good for your personal wellbeing and emotional health. I have friends and clients, who went through burnout, recovered, went back to their jobs and are now thriving. I have known others who decided that they could not go back because they did not want to go back into an environment that had crappy leadership and an unhealthy workplace culture. You have to decide what is best for you. To protect your sanity and wellbeing, sometimes you have to make a change.

5. The Principle of Reconnection

This principle has to do with seeking support. When recovering from burnout, you need a supportive tribe around you. My wife provided tremendous encouragement and support for me during my recovery, except when I talked about starting a business. She listened to me and helped me process my feelings.

I also knew I needed a support system outside of my marriage. For one, I did not want to overly burden her with my burnout condition. I also knew that I needed an outside perspective, so I put together a support group. I looked at my tribe of friends and considered who would be the people who would support, advise, encourage and be available when I needed them. I decided on five men and I want to take the time here to mention them and thank them for walking with me. Others can't walk for you in burnout, but they can walk with you. I knew I needed close friends who would walk with me. I wouldn't have survived burnout if it had not been for them.

One was Dr. Chris Craig, my college and graduate school roommate. We've been best friends for 40 years and are practically like brothers. Chuck Thompson, one of my running friends, who lives in the city where I live, is another friend whom I invited to walk with me. Chuck is great at listening, understanding and giving feedback. Chuck loves processing life and we have so much fun doing that together. Another friend was Steve Chamberlain, one of my neighbors. He and I live on the same street and we have been close friends for over 20 years. In fact, after starting my business 4 years ago, he was my first client. He is president of a small medical company.

There was also Dr. Steve Goodwin, a long-time friend, who transitioned from being a church pastor to an Organizational Development Consultant. He started his own business several years ago and has a lot of life wisdom. Last, but certainly not least, there was Mark Pendergrass, another college friend. I had not thought of him and we had not had a lot of contact over the years, but during my sabbatical, he called me, not knowing what I was going through. I explained that I was in burnout and after a few minutes into the conversation, I knew I needed him because of his empathy and understanding.

Each week, I had conversations with these men. They checked up on me, offered support, and helped me process my condition and situation. I trusted them and felt that I could be raw and vulnerable with them. They provided valuable perspective and emotional relief.

If you are in burnout and trying to recover, I recommend putting together a support group, just as I did. It is also beneficial to seek professional help and connect with a counselor. I partnered with a couple of counselors during my sabbatical, one of whom had gone through burnout himself earlier in life, so he completely understood what I was going through.

The point is you don't need to go through burnout recovery alone and you don't have to. There are people who will walk with you, support you and help you extinguish the flames of burnout in your life. You need to invest in meaningful relationships with friends, family and colleagues who understand your experience and can offer encouragement and perspective.

6. The Principle of Recreation

Up to this point, these principles seem a bit formal and structured. They probably are, but they are principles that you need to apply if you are going to successfully recover. I also encourage people who are going through burnout to plan some fun recreational activities while they are on leave. This is important because, even though you are doing some deep, intentional work to recover, you also need to have some fun. Having fun is also a healthy distraction from what you are going through. It is also good for your overall well-being.

My friend, Carl Martinez did this so well. He planned fun activities with his family and reconnected with his family. During his burnout, he was obsessed with work, and when he was with his family, he was mentally absent. During his leave of absence, he used some of that time to reconnect with his family. He and his wife also went on regular getaways together to renew and refresh their marriage.

Unfortunately, I was not able to fully apply this principle because my recovery time was between the end of May to the first of August of 2020. This was at the beginning of the COVID shutdown, so everything was closed. I was able to get creative to do some recreation with my family. My wife is a teacher, so she was doing virtual teaching at home. My youngest daughter lived with us at the time, so she also worked from home. In addition to running every day, I also took daily walks with them and we played games together in the evening.

Recreation is a great way to recharge your batteries. Doing this during a leave of absence creates the habit and rhythm of incorporating fun and recreation in your life. After you complete your leave of absence and transition back into your work, you will have learned that this needs to be a regular pattern in your life. Keep in mind that even though you are away from the stress of your normal work responsibilities, you still have accumulated stress. Recreation helps you to reduce the stress that you have accumulated from months and even years of job related stress.

What it takes to prevent burnout involves the same things that it takes to recover from burnout. Recreation releases the "feel good" hormones in your brain. These hormones help you to feel good about yourself. During burnout, people lose their sense of confidence, wellbeing and self-esteem. Recreation restores your mental and emotional resilience.

Recreation also helps you to experience quality of life. It builds healthy relationships in your family and friends. Recreation has social, mental, emotional and physical benefits. If you are in the process of recovering from burnout, make sure that you plan fun, recreational activities to engage in.

The Relapse Phenomenon

When I coach people who are in burnout, I lead them through two projects. Both of these projects require thought, reflection and intentionality. We work on a Recovery Plan and a Resilience Plan.

I do this because of the reality of the relapse phenomenon. This phenomenon is the recurrence of burnout symptoms after a period of recovery. People who have experienced and recovered from burnout have a high propensity of falling back into burnout. Research suggests that burnout relapse rates can be high. A study published in the Journal of Occupational Health found that 50% of individuals who had experienced burnout relapsed within 12 months of returning to work.

The propensity to relapse has nothing to do with physiological or genetic factors. It has to do with unresolved underlying issues. Individuals who experience burnout often do so due to a combination of work-related stressors and personal factors.

Without addressing the root causes of burnout, individuals are at risk of experiencing relapse when faced with similar stressors in the future. This is why it is important to do the reflection work and seek professional help during your recovery. Your recovery should refill your tank, but also help you identify and address the root causes so you can prevent a relapse in the future.

Other reasons for relapsing is not developing adequate coping mechanisms and stress management techniques. Effective coping mechanisms are essential for managing stress and preventing burnout. Learning stress management techniques can empower you to cope effectively with workplace stressors and reduce the risk of burnout recurrence.

People also relapse because of incomplete recovery. In some cases, individuals may return to work before fully recovering from burnout. This can increase the risk of relapse as they may not have had sufficient time to address the root causes and develop effective coping strategies.

This is why I help my clients develop a recovery plan. As I mentioned earlier, it is not enough to simply take a leave of absence and rest. You need to do the work. In the recovery plan, we use the *6 R's* to set goals and action plans that will aid in their recovery. You will also remember that what it takes to prevent burnout is what it takes to recover from burnout. My goal is not just to get my clients to recover, but to establish new rhythms in life after their recovery.

The second project is a resilience plan. This is a plan that they will use after returning to work. Many of the goals and action plans on the recovery plan will be transferred to the resilience plan. The difference is this is intended to be a life-long plan and will have additional action plans.

The resilience plan will help the person who has recovered to continue to work on those underlying issues. It is specific about coping mechanisms and stress management techniques. We look at areas such as overcommitment, perfectionism, poor boundary setting and poor self-care.

The resilience plan also addresses how to manage organizational culture factors, workload, job demands, and interpersonal relationships in the workplace. Both of these projects dive deeper into the internal factors and external factors that led to their burnout and set goals to live a quality of life that will prevent relapse.

BECOMING FULFILLED

It was Friday, August 7, 2020. I was on my way to the church to meet with the Senior Leader and chairman of the board. This meeting had been arranged following a full board session earlier in the week, where decisions regarding my return to work were discussed. Initially slated to resume duties on August 5, 2020, I received an email from the chairman of the board post-meeting, advising me to postpone my return until after our scheduled discussion. The unexpected nature of this request struck me as peculiar, a sentiment echoed by my support team, each of whom independently shared the apprehension that the board might be considering termination.

On my way to the meeting, I had a few questions ruminating in my head. *Am I going to be terminated? What is the purpose of this meeting? Are they meeting with me to discuss adjustments in my job responsibilities? If they want me to come back to my job, am I recovered enough to return to my responsibilities? A bigger question was if they had decided to reinstate me, do I really want to go back?* I was nervous about the meeting, but extremely curious about what the outcome would be.

When I arrived and entered the Senior Leader's office, I could sense that they'd already had a meeting to discuss the direction and flow of *this* meeting. I greeted both of them with a handshake and took a seat.

The chairman of the board opened the meeting by saying that the board had met and arrived at a decision. There was a pause and he then opened a folder and read a letter to me. The most memorable line in the reading of the letter was, *"The board decided that it would be inappropriate for you to return to your position, and that the termination is effective immediately."* Inappropriate?

I was shocked and hurt. I was shocked because I had done nothing wrong. I was a dedicated staff leader, who executed my job well. The church loved and appreciated my service. I didn't do anything morally wrong. Why were they terminating me? What was the reason for their decision? I felt hurt by the decision, but also by the way they were communicating with me. I was friends with both of these men. Why didn't they just have an open and frank conversation about their reservations of my returning to my position?

The letter was very formal, official and legal. They treated me like they didn't even know me. Three times I asked for a reason for my termination. They refused to answer me. All they told me was it was the board's decision. After the third time pressing for an answer, I then knew that I wasn't going to get an answer. During this exchange, the Senior Leader said nothing.

Finally, the Senior Leader spoke up. He also had a folder. He opened it and gave me termination papers that I needed to sign. I told him that I was not going to sign the papers at that time. I shared that I wanted to take them home so I could have time to carefully review them. At that moment, he also handed me a severance check. It really wasn't a true severance package. It was a payout of two weeks unused vacation. This was also very hurtful. I had gone two and a half months without a salary due to being on leave, and all they were giving me was two weeks pay? At the time, I had no prospects of another job. *How would this affect my family financially?*

I left the meeting and headed home. I called my wife to let her know about the outcome of the meeting. She was shocked and it sent her into a plethora of negative emotions. For her, the biggest emotion was fear – fear of the future. We just lost half of our income, which was a six-digit figure. She was fearful about my future career. Could my husband get another job after termination, being 56 years old and in the COVID shutdown? Who would hire him at his age and are there possibilities because so many businesses were struggling?

When I got home, I curled up into the fetal position and felt sorry for myself. I was angry, hurt, uncertain, and fearful. I was in an emotional funk for at least two weeks, trying to understand what had happened and processing all of these emotions.

After a few weeks, I became more rational. I was still experiencing the emotional funk, but I was rational enough to start thinking about my future. I have to admit that this was a setback in my recovery. Not only had I been in burnout, but now I was terminated. There was a lot to process, but I realized that I could not lie in my emotional dumpster forever. I had to move on with my life. But what would that look like? After much thought and further reflection, I decided to start a business consulting firm.

I shared the above story to set up my point that you can have a passionate life and rewarding career after burnout. I have seen different responses to burnout, but let me mention just four of them.

Ruination

Sadly, not every burnout story is a positive one. The flames of burnout have burned some people up.

Burnout has been known to ruin and destroy people. It doesn't have to come to this. If burnout victims apply and engage in some of the practices that I have talked about in the earlier chapters, they can move on to having a passionate life and career.

Unfortunately, some people who have experienced burnout have moved into what I call ruination. They don't recover, so their lives become a train wreck. They have affairs, leave their spouses, fall into deep depression, become alcoholics, fall into addictions and check out of life. Overall, burnout can have a cascading effect on every aspect of a person's life, undermining their well-being and quality of life if not addressed promptly and effectively.

Renewal

Don't be discouraged by what I said about ruination. That is only one possible outcome of people who go through burnout. By addressing your burnout and taking steps to recover, you can and will have the opposite result. I always tell people and clients that there is hope. By doing the right things and taking the proper measures, you can pull through the flames of burnout.

I have known many people who have experienced renewal. Exhaustion can be replaced with renewed energy. Apathy can be replaced with renewed passion.

Negative mindset can be replaced with a positive mindset. Emotional depletion can be replaced with a full emotional tank.

I talked about the possibility of changing jobs and careers, but some of the best success stories have been about people who recover and experience renewal and return to their original jobs. This happens because they have made both internal and external changes that allow them to go back to their jobs with a renewed sense of purpose and passion.

Rediscovery

People who adequately recover from burnout go through a period of rediscovery. They find themselves again. Their sense of identity is rediscovered. They rediscover their skills and sense of competence. They fully embrace their skills and what they are good at. They rediscover their purpose. Often when we experience job burnout, we simply go through the motions. There is no sense of purpose. Work simply is a job to be done, usually out of obligation.

Rediscovery also leads to figuring out what you really want for your life and what you want to do with your life. One of the things that I discovered after my termination was really profound. I realized that I was not only burned out in my current job, but I was also burned out in my career.

For over 30 years, I was in ministry and I was done! I came to the discovery that even if I had been reinstated by my job, the passion and sense of purpose would be missing. I further discovered that even if I had pursued and accepted another job in my career, I would not be satisfied. I was done. A part of my burnout was compassion fatigue, which not only led to exhaustion and depletion in my job, but my career overall.

Burnout is a signal that something is wrong. Going through recovery is a time of evaluation. I urge you to do some deep processing if you are in the burnout or recovery phase. Figure out what you want. What will make you happy? What will bring you the most fulfillment? What will help you live life with a sense of purpose?

Redirection

Let's revisit my story. After I was terminated from the church, I did experience depression, hurt, anger, and fear. I also felt a sense of relief because I was not going to go back to a job that I did not love and no longer enjoyed.

I was tired of working for organizations, answering to a boss, and having to report to a board. I was weary of working for bad leaders and working in unhealthy organizational cultures. I decided that I wanted to be in control of my life and work. I needed control, independence and freedom. This discovery led to redirection. My story is different than others. I did not go back to the same job with a renewed sense of purpose and passion.

This discovery led me to start my own company. One month after my termination, I incorporated, PeakePotential, Inc., which is a business consulting firm. I now do consulting, training, keynote speaking, executive coaching and writing. I have been in business now for 4 years. Not only has my new work been successful, but I am happier and more fulfilled than I have ever been professionally.

My wife has noticed a huge difference in me. She tells me that in our 35 year marriage, she has never seen me so energized and passionate about what I do. I love my life and work now. It has been said to do what you love and love what you do. That is me now. My life and career are filled with excitement, freedom and fulfillment. One of the things that I enjoy about what I do now is I feel that I am making a difference in people's lives. My closest friends have also noticed a big difference in me and they have affirmed the new direction in my life.

If you are experiencing burnout, you need to understand that there is nothing wrong with you. Burnout is prevalent and common and has become a professional epidemic. You do not have a mental illness. It is a condition or syndrome. You are simply exhausted and depleted.

If things are going well for you, especially in your career and job, I hope you will pay attention to the signs of burnout. As soon as you begin to notice some of the symptoms, address them. You need to take time to rest, reflect and regroup.

Finally, remember that burnout is temporary if you address it. Research shows that if you take the time to rest, reflect and regroup, you will recover. Be patient with yourself if you are recovering from burnout. Give yourself time to heal. You didn't get into burnout overnight. It was a gradual process. The recovery period works the same. To fully heal and recover is a process, so take the right steps to recover and be patient.

If you are in the flames of burnout, I want you to know that you are not alone. Others are suffering from it just like you. Since I have been through it, I understand where you are and I can empathize with you.

I want to close this book with a call to action. As I said earlier, others cannot walk for you through the flames of burnout, but they can walk *with* you. I want to be one who walks with you. So after reading this book, if you would like for me to coach you through your flames of burnout, reach out to me at reggie@peakepotential.com.

Thank you for reading this book. I hope it provides support, encouragement, and hope on your journey to a healthier and more fulfilled life.

AUTHOR BIO

Dr. Reggie Thomas excels in building and nurturing relationships, a skill honed through years of dedication both personally and professionally. With a fervent commitment to fostering healthy workplace dynamics and enriching personal connections, Reggie leverages his expertise to support leaders in enhancing their leadership capabilities and transforming workplace culture. Holding a doctoral degree in Leadership, Reggie conducted extensive research on the significance of Emotional Intelligence in Leadership, using his findings to empower countless leaders to improve their skills and elevate organizational morale.

As the President of PeakePotential, a firm specializing in executive coaching, leadership development, and consultancy services, Reggie channels his passion for community engagement by serving on the Board of Directors for the Chino Valley Chamber of Commerce and the Board of Trustees for California Baptist University. Additionally, he actively participates in the Rancho del Chino Rotary Club, where he serves on the Board of Directors.

A seasoned speaker with over thirty-two years of national speaking experience, Reggie offers keynote speeches, presentations, workshops, and seminars, drawing from his bestselling book, "People Pains: Fixing the Drama in Your Business." Committed to leaving a legacy of service and empowerment, Reggie finds fulfillment in witnessing the growth and achievements of others.

Outside of his professional endeavors, Reggie cherishes his role as a devoted husband to Jeannine for thirty-five years and a proud father to their two grown daughters, Amanda and Emilee. Together, Reggie and Jeannine share a passion for travel, having explored various international destinations in recent years. An avid runner, Reggie has completed forty-three marathons and six ultra-marathons, including the esteemed Boston Marathon on twelve occasions.

Dr. Reggie is also a #1 bestselling author of the book *People Pains: Fixing The Drama In Your Business*.

Learn more at: PeoplePains.com

www.ingramcontent.com/pod-product-compliance
Lightning Source LLC
LaVergne TN
LVHW051002080826
845145LV00009B/2407

* 9 7 8 1 9 4 8 3 8 2 8 6 1 *